PRACTICAL PLAYS

BY PAMELA MARX

Illustrated
by Cyd Moore

Good Year Books

Parsippany, New Jersey

Dedication
To Mark
and to my mom and dad

Good Year Books
are available for most basic curriculum subjects plus many
enrichment areas. For more Good Year Books, contact your
local bookseller or educational dealer. For a complete catalog
with information about other Good Year Books, please write:

Good Year Books
An imprint of Pearson Learning
299 Jefferson Road, P.O. Box 480
Parsippany, NJ 07054-0480
www.pearsonlearning.com
1-800-321-3106

Design by Lynne Grenier
Copyright © 1993 Pamela Marx.
All Rights Reserved.
Printed in the United States of America.

ISBN 0-673-36049-0

7 8 9 10 11 – ML – 05 04 03 02

PREFACE

Practical Plays contains six plays for performance by students in grades 1 through 5. The subject areas covered are Halloween, Thanksgiving, Winter Holiday, Valentine's Day, Brotherhood/Peace, and Earth Day-Nature.

These plays are designed to be simple enough for children with no theatrical experience. They are structured so that one or two classes can perform them with each child having only limited responsibility for learning lines. Some children can pantomime. Some can sing. The plays are also created bearing in mind the logistical limitations for play production that exist in many schools. Most of the plays can even be produced and performed within a classroom setting.

Fewer and fewer children are able to participate in theater experiences in their elementary years. This has resulted from ever-increasing budget cuts and teacher reporting and paperwork burdens that reduce available time. These plays are simple and straightforward. With a limited amount of parental help and minimal cost, they should be capable of performance in most any classroom or youth enrichment program.

Have a great time, but don't break a leg!

Acknowledgments

My grateful thanks and acknowledgment go to Marlene Culver, Debbie Mansfield, and Pamela Olson for their creativity, enthusiasm, and dedication in giving children performing opportunities and for their valuable input into the plays and ideas in this book. Additional thanks go to these teachers and to Kelly Layton, Margaret Villarreal, Deborah Davis, Marci Lawson, and Donna Scarfe, whose teaching efforts provided inspiration for many of the ideas in this book.

A special thanks goes to the students of Dahlia Heights School, and especially to Megan and Holly, for providing the inspiration for the plays in this book and ideas for improvement of many scenes and for being enthusiastic and creative actors, singers, dancers, and mimes.

Finally, my appreciation and thanks go to Mark Goldstein, Megan Goldstein, and Holly Goldstein for providing some of the writing examples included in this book.

C O N T E N T S

INTRODUCTION

Budget cuts in the educational system at all levels are bringing the curtain down on orchestras, choruses, specialty teachers, and aides who might ordinarily help support performing arts programs. Such programs offer important opportunities for children to gain experience and confidence from getting up in front of people. Nonetheless, the number of these programs is shrinking. Yet these opportunities can be among the most memorable a student takes from his or her early school years, and the most rewarding.

Moreover, for many adults, public speaking is high on their list of fears. The ability to express oneself in front of a group is invaluable to ultimate career success, regardless of one's chosen career path. Those with speaking confidence find opportunities open to them that are lost to others. The groundwork for ultimate success in this arena can and should be laid in childhood.

Experiences that a child has when young can instill the confidence upon which he or she will rely as an adult. One solitary performing experience cannot adequately provide this confidence. From repeated opportunities to perform and to speak publicly, a child experiences the sense of accomplishment that comes from a successful experience as well as the important lesson that the world doesn't come to an end if his or her part doesn't go quite as well as hoped. Both ends of the experience spectrum are important.

Plays are also an important way to drive home curriculum lessons. Plays can breathe life into history lessons, spark interest in exploration of literary characters, feelings, and attitudes, and foster investigation of world cultures and customs. Play experiences help students with other study areas as well. In rehearsing and performing plays, children enhance their reading and oral language skills.

Two other more subtle benefits result from performing plays. First, the processes of rehearsing and otherwise preparing for a play enhance student cooperation. A play is necessarily a group effort. Children learn how to be responsible for themselves as well as how to rely on and work with others. Cooperative skills are learned by doing.

A second, perhaps less tangible, benefit of classroom play production is the enhancement of the overall educational environment at a school. When one group of students performs for another, both groups of children learn. The performers learn how it feels to put themselves on the line and how they want to be treated by an audience. They learn about responsibility and teamwork. They gain poise and confidence. The students watching the performance learn, not only from the content of the play, but they also learn audience skills. They practice their listening skills. They learn to be courteous members of an audience. They also internalize the notion that if the performing students can do it, they can do it, too. Sometimes appreciative classes write letters of thanks to the performers. Sometimes the principal visits the class to express thanks and give praise. These expressions of appreciation and the cross-pollination that comes from producing plays at a school help break down the walls that sometimes isolate one class from another.

CONCERNS ABOUT PLAY PRODUCTION

Practical Plays contains six different plays, which were written to address the concerns and fears many teachers have about producing plays with children. First, their structures are flexible enough to accommodate different performance needs. Second, they are designed so that the scripts are easy to memorize. Finally, the plays contain either historical, multicultural, or other educational themes so that teachers can integrate them into a classroom curriculum. The plays in this book can be used by one class or by several classes working together. While much of the supplementary text assumes that teachers will be using this book, the activities and plays can be used with youth groups, clubs, and recreation programs.

Why are the plays in this book so easy to produce and perform? Several factors differentiate these plays from so many other plays that are written for children to perform.

- These plays can be staged in different ways so that they meet individual needs.

The plays in this book are structured so that they can be performed in a variety of ways. Flexibility is absolutely necessary when you attempt to produce an amateur play with children. Stages and staging areas vary in size and entry and exit paths. The numbers and ages of children vary. Desired lengths of performance differ. The plays in this book can be adjusted to meet these various challenges and needs. This is the primary reason these plays are called "practical."

Sometimes youth volunteers produce plays as an after-school or student enrichment opportunity. In these settings, children in grades 1 through 5 might be involved in the same production. The plays in this book can accommodate such wide differences in ages. While the plays generally specify how many characters have parts and how the parts should be split up, view these specifications as suggestions only. When your play involves children of many ages, you need to be flexible about adding lines and parts, even if those parts are really only walk-ons.

When looking at the plays and the listed character parts, remember that if you have lots of available talent, you can split up many parts to make more speaking parts possible. In addition, you can increase the number of lines in any play by including student ideas for "ad libs." Conversely, children can double up on lines if fewer actors are available, assuming the available actors are comfortable with memorizing lines. If they are not, feel free to cut out lines. Many lines in any play are not absolutely necessary to further the action. This elasticity in the number of actors necessary and, conversely, which can be accommodated, gives you tremendous flexibility. This flexibility makes undertaking the plays in this book easier than most.

- The lines in these plays are repetitive and easy.

These plays are written in such a way that the parts are not terribly demanding. Everyone, or nearly everyone, in a class or youth group can have at least one line, and you should encourage this. Sometimes children are very hesitant about asking for or taking a speaking part. If, however, children know that everyone will be given a line, even the most reserved child will step up to the mark. The more children who take and perform lines, the more who receive valuable speaking experience. For those who have more than one line, the lines are largely repetitive to make learning easy.

- The plays cover themes that reinforce classroom curriculum and behavioral standards.

The plays cover a number of different themes. They can be used for either curriculum enhancement or as holiday program material. Each play sends some sort of "moral" message, such as the value of cooperation, the fallacy of judging people on appearances, or the importance of thankfulness.

CONCERNS ABOUT COSTUMES
AND SCENERY

Don't let concerns about costumes and scenery stop you from doing a play. The plays in this book are easy to perform and stage. If costumes must be sewn and scenery must be painted, fewer rather than more plays will be performed. Therefore, "the simpler, the better" is a good motto.

Scenery is largely optional. The audience focuses its attention on the actors and what they say. Accordingly, when time, help, and resources are limited (as they usually are), don't worry about scenery.

If it's a choice between limited costuming and having scenery at all, always opt for the costumes. Children love to think about their costumes—even if they are just deciding which of their regular clothes are appropriate for a character.

While costumes of some sort should always be encouraged, they need not be a big sewing ordeal. The plays in this book often call for children to be costumed in dark pants and white shirts. Where appropriate, you can add what is best described as a "no-sew" tunic to this simple costume.

TO MAKE THE NO-SEW TUNIC:

1. Take approximately 1-1/2 to 2 yards of a half-width width of fabric (18 to 30 inches, depending upon the overall width of available fabric).

2. Fold this piece of material in half widthwise. Cut a hole for the head and a 5- to 6-inch slit down the back to allow for easy wearing.

3. Use 40- to 50-inch pieces of yarn or fabric strips to tie tunics at the waist.

This simple costume base can serve well in many contexts with only slight variation as to fabric, length, and cut. For example, a costume of dark pants, a dark no-sew tunic, white sleeves, and a white paper collar gives you an instant Pilgrim.

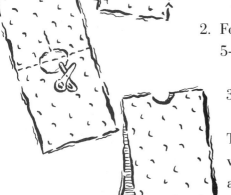

▲ **The No-Sew Tunic**

Once you decide that costumes and scenery are not an obstacle, the only real work in producing a play is the rehearsal. Children are amazingly talented, and once they learn their lines, they get their entrances and exits very quickly. Also no matter how badly rehearsals seem to go, there is seldom a bad performance. Children rise to the challenges of performance, and they focus on their tasks. They realize that "it's now or never," and they come through. They are also very helpful to one another when those momentary memory lapses occur. How can this be, you wonder, when they have sometimes been so distracted during rehearsal? It must be the smell of the greasepaint!

As you think about putting on a play without a lot of volunteer help, remember that the plays in this book are designed to be performed by a flexible number of children. Without support staff to help in play production, teachers may feel more comfortable teaming up to present a play. These plays can easily be performed by two classes working together, which can increase a teacher's comfort level substantially in taking on such a project.

You can incorporate several general activities into regular routines to help prepare children for a play experience. The activities listed below help students with performance, poise, and projection.

1. As part of the students' weekly homework, include memorization of a short poem. Each child must recite the poem on Friday of each week. Excellent poetry sources are two- to four-lined Mother Goose rhymes or the Shel Silverstein collections. There are also many other children's poetry anthologies available, which include the works of Christina Rossetti, Marchette Chute, and Robert Louis Stevenson. Ask children to memorize no more than four lines per week. Over the weeks, even the shyest children become comfortable with the process, speaking more loudly and with greater assurance and making audience eye contact.

2. Take a bit of poetry on the road. Schedule a time when children visit other classes to recite memorized poetry. Designate certain children to do introductions. The title and author of each poem should be stated. Depending on their ages, the children might want to recite the poems with hand motions that they make up. Children as old as third grade seem to enjoy this activity.

    For an alternate poetry experience, have the children invite their parents to a poetry hour. Children dress in their best party wear and recite poems as a class

as well as individually or in small groups. They learn to appreciate the rhythm, rhyme, and humor of poetry through such events.

3. Have the children present oral book reports at least once a month. This gives them a creative opportunity to decide and rehearse what they will say. They will become comfortable saying their own words in front of an audience.

    Another way to use the oral book report concept is as part of the assigned classroom reading curriculum. On a rotating basis, ask a small group of children to report orally to the class on the book just completed. Topics covered by the oral report include names and descriptions of the characters, plot outline, lessons learned from the story, and other stories to which the book is similar.

4. As part of your classroom reading program, explore character and action by having small groups of children reenact particular scenes. Remind students to discuss and decide who will play certain characters, why the characters act as they do, what lines the characters will need to say, and how to stage the reenactment. These opportunities should be informal with only two or three 20-minute sessions of class time used to prepare for the performances. Beverly Cleary books lend themselves well to this sort of activity. (You might want to give students the option of doing this activity or a group book report.)

    If equipment is available, videotape the children's scenes so that they will begin to see what happens when they don't look out at the audience, when they speak to the wall, and when they fail to enunciate and project. If some of the children have video cameras at home, perhaps you can assign extra credit projects in which groups of children create and tape a play version of a book or a book chapter at home.

5. For older children, develop a storytelling program with a class of younger children. Perhaps the younger class can be the group with whom you ultimately perform a play. Older children read stories aloud to the younger class according to a schedule upon which the teachers agree. Particularly advanced upper-graders might develop pantomime activities for their audiences as part of the storytelling activity. Storytellers learn to speak clearly and project their voices.

6. Use pantomime as part of classroom activities. Have pantomime sessions in which children explore feelings, sports, jobs, and daily activities (such as preparing for school—dressing, combing hair, or brushing teeth). The sessions

can be structured as class activities, a charades-type game, or a paired activity in which students pantomime to each other.

7. Plan demonstration days. Tell children they will each have three to five minutes to demonstrate how to do something, such as how to tie a bow; lace shoes; make a ring from a dollar bill; fold a simple origami animal; mix instant pudding; stuff, stamp, and address an envelope; or frost a cupcake. They need to decide what to demonstrate, the materials needed, and the steps involved in the process. They can demonstrate as individuals or in pairs. Encourage them to rehearse the demonstration at least two or three times at home.

   Schedule demonstration days for every Friday in a given month. Remind children to speak loudly and to make eye contact with the audience. You might want to allow for a short question and answer period at the end of each demonstration.

8. Ask your parent organization to sponsor an event at which students are encouraged to perform using their voices, their feet, or actual musical instruments as their "instrument." Call this program of recitations, song, and dance simply an "Instrument Night." With one organizational meeting to determine who plans to perform, the event can take place with a minimum of fuss. Have student performers sit in the first rows of the audience. When their names are announced, they can walk to the stage to make their presentations. After their acts, they return to their seats. This event is not like a typical school talent show in which many students lip-sync popular rock and rap tunes. Such acts should not be included in an "Instrument Night," but should be reserved for an all-school talent event.

PREPARING THE CHILDREN

There are several stages involved in putting on a play, and they all occur within about a three-week period. During this period children go from the initial introduction of the play to actual performance. Each chapter in this book provides:

- ideas for oral or active performing exercises specifically designed to prepare children to perform the play in that chapter
- writing activities to help insure that students' experience with the play is a complete language arts adventure
- cross-curricular activities involving art, science, and/or cooking to help make the characters, actions, and meanings of the plays more tangible to the students

The performing, writing, and other cross-curricular activities can be integrated into classroom routine from the time you introduce the play to the children. In this way, you integrate the play experience thematically into the curriculum and the educational value of the play is significantly enhanced.

In addition to the preparatory ideas included in each chapter, the following "how-to" list provides you with detailed guidelines applicable to preparing children for performing any play, regardless of the subject matter. This how-to list gives you detailed suggestions for ways in which to undertake the play process, beginning with the first reading of the play through rehearsal and final performance.

GETTING "REHEARSAL READY"

1. Give the children copies of the play and read it with them. Answer any questions about the action. At this point, randomly assign parts (let the children know that these are not the final parts). Go through several reads of the play. Use these read-throughs to get a sense of the appropriate part for each child.

2. If a play does not have enough lines for all the children involved, let the children look for places in the play where new lines can be added. Children in Grade 3 and up are very good at this and come up with very creative and interesting part additions to make a play better than written.

3. The next step is to assign parts. For any parts critical to the action of the play, have two sets of actors or a group of actors cover the parts so that, if one is ill, another can step in. For example, in the Thanksgiving play, the characters of Pilgrims Mary and Thomas are critical to the action. Assign two actors to each of these parts and they can share the lines. If one is missing, the remaining actor can fill in the lines.

    In assigning parts, structure the assignment process with the personality of your group in mind. With some groups, you can solicit interest for certain high-visibility parts. If you have multiple volunteers, draw numbers to determine who gets the parts. With some groups, it is easier to make the part decision on the basis of the children's responses to the play read-throughs.

4. Once you assign parts, have the children read through the play aloud. Remind the children to learn to recognize the line or action that immediately precedes each of their lines. This exercise helps each child better understand the flow of the play and the way in which his or her part fits into the overall structure of the play.

5. If your play or assembly performance includes songs, begin to incorporate these songs into your classroom routine. Set aside some time to work on the songs over and above actual on-stage rehearsal time. If you have a weekly poetry memorization program, use parts of the lyrics as your poems from week to week. In order to teach the children the song melody, sing the song for them or, if you have a volunteer who can make an audiotape of the song, play the song for them. To teach an unfamiliar melody, work phrase by phrase. (Most of the songs suggested in this book, however, are sung to familiar melodies to facilitate song learning.)

Play the songs as much as possible and have children sing along. This can be done at art time, for example. If you lead a choral group who will be singing the songs for your performance, you may want a more polished sound. In that case, use a slightly more rigorous rehearsal technique. If you hear bad notes during rehearsal, go over the problem phrase two or three times as a group. If the problem persists, ask the children to sing the phrase in groups of three to try to isolate the melody problem.

6. Ask children to begin thinking about any props they need or want for the play. Also, ask them what kind of scenery they would suggest. Have at hand your own ideas for scenery, or draw ideas from the suggestions in this book.

These questions have two purposes. First, they get the children involved in actively thinking about the action of the play and in feeling responsible for the production. Second, children are very creative and their suggestions may lead you to good ideas for scenery or staging that you had not considered.

7. About seven to ten days after rehearsals start, keep up the children's excitement by having them make some or all of the following:

- Design posterboard posters to advertise the play. Include the play title, the classes or groups participating, and the date, time, and place of performance. Hang the posters in high-visibility locations around school.
- Have students write invitations to their parents. Use this as an opportunity to introduce or reinforce basic principles of letter writing.
- Create an all-class invitation to send to other classes and staff members at the school. Copy the final product and distribute it. Perhaps students will want to hand-deliver the invitations and make short oral presentations to invite individual classes to the play.

REHEARSAL TIME

As much as possible, hold rehearsals in the staging area. The "stage" can be in an auditorium, cafeteria, multipurpose room, gymnasium, or even a classroom. When you can't rehearse in the staging area, try to rehearse in an area of the same approximate size. In a facility with no formal staging area, be creative about finding your stage. Any flat area big enough to hold your actors and allow for entry and exit paths will do. Obviously, such a space can be at the end of a classroom. With desks pushed slightly back and desk aisles used as entry and exit paths from the stage area, a classroom can serve very well for a performance involving a single class.

Most rehearsal schedules (the period of time during which children are actually rehearsing on stage) should be no longer than two to three weeks, assuming you are able to rehearse three or four times a week for thirty minutes to an hour each time. At the end of two or two-and-a-half weeks, children will be peaking. They are familiar with their parts and, usually, all the other actors' parts as well. They are beginning to get a little blasé about rehearsals because they "already know how to do this." It's time to perform!

If you are rehearsing a play only once a week as an after-school enrichment opportunity, you will need to rehearse students for five to seven weeks so they will be adequately prepared. You will need an extra meeting or two if students will be making the scenery or costumes.

REHEARSAL TIPS

1. Use your first rehearsal to set the tone for all the rehearsals to come. Use encouraging words to enhance performance volume and clarity. Remind the children to be courteous listeners when other actors are on stage. Occasionally, you will need to verbally chastise the children when they goof around, but if you let children know ahead of time what is expected of them, you should not have any serious discipline problems.

2. At the first rehearsal do a single complete run-through of the play. Let children use their scripts. Use this rehearsal to begin to work out kinks in your staging ideas (actor locations, entrances and exits, scenery logistics). Sometimes the actors won't fit where you thought they would. Sometimes the stage looks too bare or too crowded. Make these adjustments in the first few rehearsals.

3. During the first rehearsal, children often forget to say their lines on cue. Before you begin, remind them to think about their cues—what line or event comes immediately before they are to say their lines or make stage entrances or exits.

4. At the first two or three rehearsals, keep all actors in front of the curtain (if there is a curtain or backstage area). Even if the actors will ultimately enter the stage from backstage, keep them in front for these rehearsals. In the first few rehearsals, run-throughs take longer than they do as you approach performance. This is because you stop and start when things aren't working quite right. If the actors in a scene are having trouble, and you have adult help, take that group (all of whom are part of the same scene or sequence of lines) to another room to do a mini-rehearsal while the general rehearsal proceeds.

5. During each rehearsal, focus on the following instructional ideas:

- **Constantly remind children to project.** Do not let children rely on microphones. The only part in any play for which a microphone should be used is that of the narrator, if the play calls for one. Children as young as first grade can project loudly enough for their voices to be heard in a 150- to 200-seat auditorium. As you rehearse children, adopt a simple signal they can look for to let them know that they need to speak up. An easy signal is raising your hand to your ear when you can't hear.

- **Remind children to speak slowly.** Children always want to rush through their lines and bound off stage. Emphasize slow, loud speech. If children are speaking loudly enough, they are usually speaking slowly enough. Let a child shorten his or her lines if that helps the child slow down and speak loudly.

- **Once parts are assigned, let the children use their scripts for the first or second run-through only.** The sooner they stop relying on paper, the sooner they learn their parts, project their voices, and raise their eyes from the floor. This simple no-script rule imposes a not-so-subtle pressure on the children to take responsibility for learning their lines.

- For those children who have more than one or two lines (and even for those with only a line or two), **make sure they understand that the scripted lines can be adjusted.** If it is easier for the child to say something different that gets the same message across, this is just fine. It also gives the child a controlled and unthreatening creative opportunity.

Allowing for adjustment of lines is especially important with older children, particularly children with larger parts. Let them know that they can work out the exact words; that the script is really a guideline. They should be comfortable with what they are saying. Most importantly, they should understand what they are saying. If they understand it better in words of their own choosing, so be it. This flexibility gives them a good sense of control over the lines and a sense of the value of their ideas and input.

SUMMING UP

Producing plays often intimidates adults and children alike. We worry about costumes, scenery, rehearsals, lights, and curtains. We get bogged down. Because the list of "musts" is so long, we stop before we get started.

Don't let the peripherals hold you back. The most important things in a play are the actors and their lines. Everything else is gravy. If you have time for curtains and scenery, that's great, but you can produce a play very successfully without these extras.

Peruse this selection of plays with a flexible frame of mind. Remember the motto "the simpler, the better." A few years from now you might be surprised at the number of plays you have produced with the children you teach or supervise. And the benefits to those children will be significant and long term. Although you may not be able to see or easily quantify them now, you will have made many contributions to their development.

THE HAUNTING CONTEST

This play uses a Halloween story to relay principles of cooperation. It uses the classic Halloween characters of witches, ghosts, scarecrows, and jack-o'-lanterns to move the plot line along. In "The Haunting Contest," the Goblin Council must decide who will get the opportunity to haunt on Halloween. Should it be the speedy witches or the bright jack-o'-lanterns? Perhaps the noisy ghosts or the scary scarecrows should have the chance? The Goblin Council decides that, to have a successful Halloween haunt, all the goblins must work together.

WHY SHOULD CHILDREN PERFORM THIS PLAY?

This play takes typical Halloween characters and places them in a situation in which they must all work together to have a successful Halloween haunt. There are several reasons why you might want to perform this play.

First, the lines in this play rhyme. Performing a play that has repeating rhymes reinforces the sounds and rhythms of verse. It can reinforce classroom lessons on verse and rhyming as well as serve as a jumping-off point for written rhyming exercises.

Second, many of the lines are recited or sung by characters in groups in unison. As such, this play may serve as a less intimidating introduction to play performance than a play in which all children speak individual lines.

Third, this play involves three performance skills—recitation, song, and a limited amount of dance. As such, it is an opportunity for children to perform in several media as part of one effort.

Finally, the theme of the play is cooperation. Since Halloween falls early in the school year, this theme is a good one for that time of year. As children start the year, teachers try to instill a disciplined, but cooperative, spirit in their students. Through rehearsal and performance, this play will reinforce those behavioral standards at a critical point in the school year.

The Haunting Contest
A Halloween Play

How should I prepare children for performing this play?

Halloween is an exciting time of year for elementary-school children. They enjoy the art of the season, the stories, and the prospect of dressing up. Performing the play in this chapter helps channel some of that energy. Concurrent with the preparation process for performing the play, classroom activities can include thematic art, cooking, and math activities that involve the major character groups of the play and writing activities that reinforce both rhyming skills and creative thinking.

PERFORMING ACTIVITIES

The suggested activities in this section are designed to help children with their acting responsibilities in "The Haunting Contest." When undertaken together with some of the other preparatory activities suggested in the Introduction, they give students a good grounding in the performance skills needed for this play.

▲ **Character Pantomime**

1. **Sing Along.** Prepare children for the songs in this play. There are six different songs, which are all sung to familiar melodies, to move the action along. Each song's words can also be chanted. To help children learn the words to the songs, ask them to memorize the lyrics of the songs for weekly poetry recitations. If the children will be chanting rather than singing the songs during performance, ask that they prepare their recitations with inflection and dramatic effect. They can work in character groups to do this. If children will be singing and you have a tape of the recorded songs, play this tape during art, craft, and clean-up times to reinforce the words and how the words fit with the melodies.

2. **Character Pantomime.** Engage children in pantomime exercises that help them explore the characters in the play. Scarecrows should be wiggly; their arms shimmy and shake and their knees bend so that they undulate up and down. Witches stir a big pot of brew. Jack-o'-lanterns sway from side to side slowly and stiffly; they can adopt funny faces and such other attitudes indicated by the lyrics of their song. Ghosts sway and wave their arms about in an eerie way. Take two-to five-minute pantomime breaks from time to time to let children work on their pantomime skills. As you identify children with particularly effective panto-mime ideas, have them demonstrate these in groups of three or four in front of the class.

3. **How-To Presentations.** Adapt the Demonstration Day idea to your Halloween classroom activities. If children will be creating witch or ghost art or building scarecrows, ask groups to work together to analyze the project as to steps

From *Practical Plays*, published by GoodYearBooks. Copyright ©1993 Pamela Marx.

involved and materials needed. Then ask each group to make an oral presentation to the class, telling about the manner in which to make the chosen art project.

4. **Dramatic Reading.** Use Jack Prelutsky's *It's Halloween* collection or another spooky Halloween poetry collection as the basis for some short class dramatic readings. With dramatic readings, children learn to project, read with expression, and speak clearly. They need not memorize the poems. Rather, they familiarize themselves with the poems at home and read them to classmates or to younger children. Have the children work in groups of two or three. When presenting poems, each child needs a copy of the poem. The children need to decide ahead of time which student will read which lines, which lines they will all read together, and whether they can use hand motions for dramatic effect.

WRITING ACTIVITIES

Writing exercises are another way to introduce and reinforce the characters of the play. Here are some simple ideas:

1. **Halloween Limericks.** Ask children to write goblin limericks. To reinforce the concept of rhyming, ask each child to make up a limerick about his or her favorite Halloween goblin or activity. The rhyme and meter schemes for a limerick are as follows:

-/-/-/ A	or	- -/- -/- -/ A	or a combination of these
-/-/-/ A		- -/- -/- -/ A	
-/-/ B		- -/- -/ B	
-/-/ B		- -/- -/ B	
-/-/-/ A		- -/- -/- -/ A	

Example:

There once was a ghost named Sam
Who ate only beans and ham
When he flew in the air
He lost all his hair
And his face turned the color of jam.

▲ A Ghostkin

2. **Dual Monsters.** Have children write about "dual monsters." A dual monster combines two goblins, animals, or monsters to create a new species. Each child should write a paragraph identifying the two entities that make up the dual monster, something about how it lives that combines characteristics of both, and any dangerous characteristics that result from the monsterly mutation. If you choose, two students can work together. In this case, each child selects his or her own monster and together they decide how their dual monster will work.

Example: Ghostkin

A ghostkin is part ghost and part pumpkin. He is orange all over with large jack-o'-lantern eyes. His jack-o'-lantern mouth yells "boo" late at night. Beware if you see a ghostkin rattling chains at midnight because, if he sees you, he will chase you and turn you into his favorite food—pumpkin pie.

Encourage children to draw pictures of their dual monsters.

3. **R.I.P. Tombstones.** As both an art and writing project, have children make tombstones. To make a tombstone, cut an 18-inch-long tombstone shape out of black construction paper. Cut a slightly smaller sheet of lined paper to glue onto the black tombstone (so that the black tombstone frames the lined sheet). On the lined sheet, the writer writes his or her Rest in Peace statement, or eulogy, for a toy or shoe or other object that has broken or "died."

Example: R.I.P.

My favorite jacket with a baseball on it died October 10, 1991. I left it on the playground overnight. When I went to find it, it was gone—never to be seen again.

This eulogy should specify the mourned item, the date of loss, and the manner of "death." RIPs can be much longer than this example if the writer has a creative streak. You might want to require a minimum of five or seven sentences.

4. **Friendly Ghosts for a Bulletin Board.** Make a friendly ghost bulletin board. It reinforces the cooperative theme of the play and requires that children work together. Have children work in pairs. Each child in the pair traces the other child's hand on white construction paper and cuts it out. The palm becomes the head of the ghost. Children can make a ghost face on the palm. Under the face they can write "I like (partner's name) because_____." In each of the five

fingers, the child writes one thing he or she likes about his or her partner. This project can also be done by tracing around the partner's shoe or sock to make the ghost.

CROSS-CURRICULAR ACTIVITIES

The play has four main Halloween character groups. These are witches, ghosts, scarecrows, and jack-o'-lanterns. Children can do several art and related cooking activities during the rehearsal weeks to reinforce the characters. Some ideas for these activities are:

1. **"Fast Flying" Witches.** To make the witch, you need:

    two sheets of newspaper
    a 16-inch square of black tissue paper
    a 7-inch diameter circle of black construction paper
    markers
    yarn

▲ **A "Fast Flying" Witch**

-   Crumple one piece of newspaper into a tight ball. This will be the head.
-   Place the head in the center of the remaining sheet of newspaper and draw the sheet up around the head, gathering it together at the "neck." The remainder of the sheet hangs down and becomes the witch body or dress. Tie yarn around the neck.
-   Accordion-fold or gather the tissue paper about two inches from one end. Tie this to the neck to create the witch's cape.
-   Use markers or scraps of paper to make a face.
-   Cut the black paper circle from one edge to the center. Overlap the open ends to form a cone, and glue the ends to make a hat. Glue the hat to the witch's head. If you like, you can add a broom by attaching fringed yellow paper to the end of a straw. Insert the broom in the witch's dress. Hang the witch from the strings around the witch's neck.

Give your good witches a spider treat—spider cupcakes made from cupcakes, chocolate frosting, brown pipecleaners, and assorted candies like jelly beans, gumdrops, peanuts, or candy corn.

To make this treat, first prepare and bake the cupcakes. Then cut the pipecleaners in thirds. Children can frost the cupcakes and decorate them with candies for spider eyes and designs. Give each child eight pipecleaners for legs. He or she can bend the pipecleaners into zigzags and then place four on each side of his or her cupcake. The cupcake spider is complete.

2. **Gauze Ghosts.** For each ghost you need:

an empty soda bottle
golf ball, golf practice ball, or Ping Pong ball
16" x 16" square of gauze fabric or cheesecloth
starch or white glue and water
black construction-paper eyes

- Place the golf ball on the mouth of the bottle. Cover the ball and bottle with waxed paper and use rubber bands to hold the paper to the bottle.
- Take fabric and dip it into starch or a mixture of one part white glue and one part water. Squeeze the excess fluid from the cloth and drape it over the bottle so that it hangs evenly. Let dry. (You might want to place the bottle and ghost on waxed paper as you make it so you can remove it easily when dry.)
- Glue on black construction-paper eyes.

For younger children, waxed-paper ghosts might be easier. Cut out a basic ghost shape from two sheets of waxed paper. Paint starch onto the first waxed sheet. Lay black paper eyes and white tissue paper squares on the starch. Press the second sheet on top. When dry, the sheets stick together. Or you can use the ironing method to make this ghost: Place the black construction-paper eyes and mouth on one sheet of waxed paper and squares of white tissue paper randomly, if desired. Cover with a second sheet of waxed paper and iron together. Hang these ghosts from the ceiling.

Ghost cupcakes are a fun food activity for children. First, frost a cupcake with white frosting. Use dabs of frosting to affix two chocolate chips to a large marshmallow. These are the ghost's eyes. Place the decorated marshmallow atop the frosted cupcake. Your ghost is complete.

3. **Life-Sized Scarecrows.** Most city children have no sense of what a scarecrow is or its purpose. For such children, making a life-sized scarecrow can be great fun. This is a good activity for the end of October as it then serves to decorate your classroom through the harvest month of November. To make a life-sized scarecrow:

▲ **Gauze Ghost**

From *Practical Plays*, published by GoodYearBooks. Copyright ©1993 Pamela Marx.

- Use two 1" x 2" pieces of wood—24 and 30 inches in length, respectively. Nail the two pieces together in a cross shape so that about 3 inches of the 30-inch piece protrudes above the cross piece. The 24-inch piece serves as the shoulder frame. The protruding 3-inch section will be the part of the frame to which you tie the head.

- You will need a large stack of newspapers, a long-sleeved shirt, and long pants to create the body of your scarecrow. Use newspaper to stuff a yard-diameter circle of burlap cloth or a medium-sized paper bag for the head. A hat is always a good idea. If you have no hat, glue yarn to the head for hair. (Tacky glue works better for this than plain white glue.)

- Sew or pin the shirt to the pants so that the shirt is tucked inside the pants. Use yarn to tie off the sleeves and pant cuffs. Unbutton the shirt and place the t-shaped frame inside the clothing. Stuff the entire body, including limbs, with crumpled newspaper. Button the shirt closed.

- If all the children are working on one scarecrow as a class project, have small groups work on decorating particular clothing items before you put the scarecrow together. Using fabric scraps, children can glue "patches" onto the shirt and pants with tacky glue to create a patchwork scarecrow. Another group can work on the head and face. There should be enough work to allow every child to play a little part in putting your scarecrow together. Again, since this is a cooperative activity, it reinforces in an active way the theme of the play.

For an alternate scarecrow project, make the frame by rolling newspaper and tying two lengths of rolled newspaper together in a cross shape. Use paper bags or plastic garbage bags for the clothing. Stuff a paper bag with newspaper for the head. This can even be a "recycling" scarecrow, since most of the articles that comprise it are recyclable.

▼ **Decorate a Pumpkin!**

4. **Pumpkin Activities.** Ask each child to bring a pumpkin to class. Use some of the pumpkins for one activity and some for another. Here are some ideas:

DECORATE A PUMPKIN

Rather than carving pumpkins into jack-o'-lanterns, decorate them into Jacks, Janes, and Jimmys. Using permanent markers, construction paper, yarn, and cloth, children can create pumpkin people individually, or they can work together in groups to create their pumpkin people.

PUMPKINS BY THE POUND

The weighing and sorting of pumpkins by size can be a fun and interesting learning experience. The group can also graph or plot distribution of pumpkin sizes. Another exercise involves the counting of seeds contained in one or two pumpkins. And don't forget, you can wash the seeds and roast them for snacking, if you like. To do this, wash them and soak them in lightly salted water for an hour. Let them dry. Place them on a non-stick cookie sheet and bake in the oven at 375° until lightly brown.

PUMPKIN TREATS

There are many great recipes for pumpkin breads, pumpkin pie, and pumpkin muffins. You can bake up fresh pumpkin and puree it in a blender or use canned pumpkin for these recipes. For starters, the exercise of simply cutting and baking pumpkin can be a different experience for children. We often forget that pumpkin is simply squash. Sliced into 2-inch pieces and baked at 350° until tender, pumpkin is a very tasty vegetable. Serve it with butter or margarine and a little brown sugar.

If you prefer baked goods, here's a good muffin or bread recipe:

1 cup margarine or butter	1 tsp. baking soda
2-1/3 cups powdered sugar	2 tsps. cinnamon
3 eggs	1 tsp. ground clove
2 cups pumpkin	1/2 tsp. nutmeg
3-2/3 cups flour	1/2 tsp. salt
1/2 tsp. baking powder	

- Cream the butter and sugar. Add eggs and beat.
- Add the pumpkin and mix well.
- Mix all dry ingredients, and then slowly mix this into the creamed mixture.
- Bake in two greased loaf pans or paper-lined muffin tins at 325° until done—about an hour for breads, less for muffins.

You can jazz up this recipe a bit by adding 1/2 cup chopped nuts, chocolate chips, butterscotch chips, or all three.

5. **"All Character" Art.** You might try a crayon-resist art project that allows children to explore any or all of the play's characters in one project. Have

children create Halloween scenes with crayon on white construction paper. Remind children to press hard and to use lots of bright crayon colors, such as yellow, orange, white, red, purple, and green. Challenge children to create Halloween scenes that include each of the characters from the play. For example, pumpkins grow next to a scarecrow while ghosts and a witch fly through the air. Once the crayon pictures are complete, children paint over their pictures with slightly thinned black paint. The crayon designs "resist" the black paint and show through for a striking finished effect.

How should i stage this play?

The staging of this play is relatively straightforward. Mandatory props are limited to a table and chairs for the council and king, a gavel, and the criers' scrolls. Each group of actors enters, performs, and exits, leaving a clear path for the goblins that follow. The number of goblins in each group can vary to accommodate available children.

COSTUMES

Costuming for this play is simple. Some costuming suggestions are provided below. Stay away from face masks, as they will undermine the children's lines and songs. You might want to use some limited face paint if you have help to apply it.

Goblin Council: Dress in any sort of silly, crazy day or goblin clothes. The king wears a construction-paper crown. Alternately, have council members wear large, white-paper collars over dark clothing. The collars can be cut out of butcher paper and shaped like Pilgrim collars. (See page 38 for directions for making collars.)

Village Crier: Dress in any sort of silly or ghoulish clothes. Funny hair and face paint is optional. Alternatively, criers can dress like goblin council members.

Scarecrows: Wear plaid shirts and jeans and old hats. Face paint, such as triangle eyes and big mouths, is appropriate.

Jack-o'-Lanterns: Wear dark clothing. Hang large orange tagboard jack-o'-lanterns from necks or use orange unbelted no-sew tunics with eyes and mouth drawn on with markers.

Witches: Dress in all dark colors, preferably black or a combination of black, purple, and green. Add black construction-paper hats. Cut 3-foot-diameter circles from black cloth, and add head holes and back slits for witch capes.

Ghosts: Dress all in white with white crêpe streamers pinned at the shoulders. Or you can staple white streamers to pipecleaner necklaces and armbands. Wear silly hats, if desired. A black plastic derby or top hat looks good. White no-sew tunics can also be used here with large black construction-paper eyes attached with glue or safety pins. A child could also wear an oversized t-shirt or Dad's old white dress shirt.

SCENERY

You can handle scenery in a couple of ways. For a simple approach, merely hang some of your classroom art around the stage or pin it onto the curtains. Drape the table or throne with black or orange cloth.

For something slightly more dramatic, but still easy, cut large white paper ghost shapes (four to five feet tall) and affix these to the stage or curtains. Cut out large black construction-paper eyes and mouths to decorate the ghosts. Another scenery idea is to cover the back of the stage with black paper that is decorated with a large moon and foil stars. Finally, depending upon the background of the stage area, simply decorate it with pairs of eyes cut out of black construction paper, hanging them randomly on the stage background.

THE HAUNTING CONTEST STUDENT SCRIPT

PLAYERS

Goblin Councilpeople (1 to 19)

Goblin King

Village Criers (1 to 6)

Witch Leaders (1 or 2)

Group of Witches (as many as desired)

Group of Jack-o'-Lanterns (as many as desired)

Group of Scarecrows (as many as desired)

Group of Ghosts (as many as desired)

Ghost Leaders (1 or 2)

Scarecrow Leaders (1 or 2)

Jack-o'-Lantern Leaders (1 or 2)

PROPS

Table

Gavel

Chairs

Six Scrolls (one for each Crier)

Note: If you have twenty councilpeople, have them sit in two rows, one behind the other. Criers stand behind councilpeople, each holding a large scroll. If you have few councilpeople, seat them at a large table.

Curtain rises.

All Goblins (Scarecrows, Ghosts, Jack-o'-Lanterns, and Witches) enter from side, dancing and singing (or chanting) the "Goblin Song." If space is limited, this group can include two or three members of each goblin group while the remaining actors of each group remain offstage.

Dancing can be simply bouncing about in a lively fashion without taking any steps.

Goblin Song (sung to the tune of "The Farmer in the Dell"):

Goblins all are we.

Yes, goblins all are we.

We haunt for Halloween,

'cause goblins all are we.

We haunt with glee.
Yes, we haunt with glee.
Boo, hiss, and ha ha hee,
Oh, we haunt with glee.

Goblins stop dancing and start to sit as Crier begins to call. If stage area will not accommodate all seated goblins, then have all goblins except the Witches exit. Witches will be seated.

Crier 1 (stands with scroll as if reading)
Hear ye, hear ye, listen to me.
The Goblin Council will now convene.
(sits)

Goblin King pounds gavel.

Councilperson 1
We hear you, Crier, we hear your words.

Councilperson 2
What is the question to be heard?

Crier 2 (standing)
The question, your honors, please lend an ear,
Is who gets to haunt Halloween this year?
(sits)

Councilperson 3
We hear you, Crier. Now take your place.

Councilperson 4
Goblins, step up and state your case.

Crier 3 (standing)
Calling the witches, calling them now.
Step up to the king and sing out loud.
(sits)

Witches stand and gather at center stage. Movements may be choreographed for them or they can merely state lines and sing. You might choose to have all but two or three remain stationary. Those chosen as dancers can make some hurried movements, such as broom-flying to the beat of the song.

(Note: The lines of Witch Leaders 1 and 2 can be stated instead by all witches in unison.)

Witch Leader 1
We are the witches of Halloween.

Witch Leader 2
The fastest goblins to be seen.

All Witches commence singing Witches' Song. They pantomime stirring a witch's brew.

Witches' Song (sung to the tune of "Alouette")

We're the witches
Flying on our broomsticks
We're the witches
We can fly so quick
We can fly. We do not lie.
Watch us zoom up to the sky.
To the sky
We don't lie
Ohhh . . . .
(Repeat first four lines.)

Alternate Witches' Song (sung to the tune of "Jim Along Josie"):

Since it is time for Halloween now,
Let's make haste and plan our flight.
Yes, it is time for Halloween now.
We will have such fun tonight.

Jump on our broomsticks
Lickety split. Let's
Jump on our broomsticks
To scare your wits.

(Optional or Alternate Verse)

Zoom, zoom on our broomsticks
Zip, zip, zap.
Zoom, zoom on our broomsticks
Zip, zip, zap.

Witches cackle and stop singing and dancing, but remain standing.

Councilperson 5

We thank you, witches, for your words,

Councilperson 6

But the other goblins must now be heard.

Witches hunch over with disappointed "ohhhs" and "ahhhs" and exit.

Crier 4 (standing)

Calling the ghosts, calling them now.
Step up to the king and sing out loud.
(sits)

Ghosts enter or stand and take center stage area. They may sing and dance to choreographed steps, if desired.

(Note: The lines of Ghost Leaders 1 and 2 can be stated by the Ghosts in unison instead.)

Ghost Leader 1

We are the ghosts of Halloween,

Ghost Leader 2

The loudest goblins to be seen.

All Ghosts make assorted loud booing sounds waving arms around. Then they commence singing "Ghost Song."

Ghost Song (sung to the tune of "Frère Jacques"):

We go haunting, we go haunting
Everywhere, everywhere.
We can frighten anyone, we can frighten anyone,
So beware, so beware.

As we're haunting, as we're haunting
We call out, we call out
Louder and louder, louder and louder.
Hear us shout, hear us shout.

Ghosts boo and ooh and sway.

Councilperson 7
We thank you, ghosts, for your words,

Councilperson 8
But the other goblins must now be heard.

Ghosts hunch over dejectedly, ooohing and ahhhing as they exit.

Crier 5 (standing)
Calling the scarecrows, calling them now.
Step up to the king and sing out loud.
(sits)

Scarecrows enter or stand and take center stage. They should walk "wiggly all over."

(Note: The lines of Scarecrow Leaders 1 and 2 can be stated by the Scarecrows in unison instead.)

Scarecrow Leader 1
We are the scarecrows of Halloween,

Scarecrow Leader 2
The scariest goblins to be seen.

Scarecrows sing "Scarecrow Song." They may wiggle or dance, if desired.

Scarecrow Song (sung to the tune of "Sing a Song of Sixpence")

Can you guess who we are?
Scarecrows all are we.
Aren't we just the scariest
Goblins to be seen?

We can look so sour.
We can look so mad.
We can scare most anyone
And that makes us so glad.
> *(Repeat, if desired.)*

Councilperson 9
We thank you, scarecrows, for your words.

Councilperson 10
But the other goblins must now be heard.

Scarecrows exit dejectedly.

Crier 6 (standing)
Calling the jack-o'-lanterns, calling them now.
Step up to the king and sing out loud.

Jack-o'-lanterns enter or stand and take center stage. They may dance to song, if desired.

(Note: The lines of Jack-o'-Lantern Leaders 1 and 2 can be stated by the Jack-o'-Lanterns in unison instead.)

Jack-o'-Lantern Leader 1
We are the jack-o'-lanterns of Halloween,

Jack-o'-Lantern Leader 2
The brightest goblins to be seen.

Jack-o'-Lanterns sing the "Jack-o'-Lantern Song."

Jack-o'-Lantern Song (sung to the tune of "O Tannenbaum"— *slowly with bodies swaying from side to side*):

We jack-o'-lanterns march along
Though all the night is darkness.
We smile as brightly as we can
To scare whoever passes.

Oh, we can jump and we can scream,
But it's our smile that is so mean.
We look this way and then look that,
We even scare the old black cat.

> *(Repeat first two lines of first verse.)*

Councilperson 11

We thank you, jack-o'-lanterns, for your words.

Councilperson 12

Now all the goblins have been heard.

> *Jack-o'-Lanterns sit down. If Witches, Ghosts, and Scarecrows have already left the stage, they reenter now and find a seat. Councilpeople are conferring with one another. These actors pantomime whispering and talking as though they are deciding who should haunt Halloween. They all begin to nod heads as if in agreement when the Goblin King hits the gavel and calls the council to order.*

Goblin King (hitting gavel)

Come to order. Come to order.

> *Goblin King indicates with the head or hand for Councilperson 13 to proceed. Councilperson 13 nods back and begins.*

Councilperson 13

We've heard the facts, you state them well.
Now we must decide, and time will tell.

Councilperson 14

The witches looked speedy from where we sat
But we need more for Halloween than that.

Councilperson 15

The ghosts were loud from where we sat
But we need more for Halloween than that.

Councilperson 16

The scarecrows looked scary from where we sat
But we need more for Halloween than that.

Councilperson 17

The jack-o'-lanterns looked bright from where we sat
But we need more for Halloween than that.

Councilperson 18

So here's our choice, we tell you true

Councilperson 19

We need you all or it just won't do!

Goblin King

So come all you goblins, let's all join in
And make this our very best Halloween.

All Goblins stand up and cheer. They assemble in their particular goblin group and as they sing they walk around, mix up, and join hands.

All Goblins sing closing song. Councilpeople, Goblin King, and Criers watch the festivities.

Closing Song (sung to the tune of "Shortnin' Bread"—*happily, with spirit, holding hands*):

We are the goblins of Halloween.
Each of us has got a part to play in the scene.
Some of us are loud and some of us are bright.
Some of us are fast but we're together tonight.

We will haunt your houses,
We will haunt your parks.
We will be so scary when it gets dark.

So, beware, get ready,
Here we come.
So, beware, get ready,
We'll have some fun.

(Repeat all or part of song as desired.)

Curtain Falls.

THE END

SUGGESTED READINGS

Baba Yaga by Ernest Small. Houghton Mifflin, 1966.

Barn Dance by Bill Martin, Jr., and John Archambault. Henry Holt and Company, 1985.

Bunnicula by Deborah Howe. Atheneum, 1979.

The Ghost-Eye Tree by Bill Martin, Jr., and John Archambault. Henry Holt and Company, 1985.

It's Halloween by Jack Prelutsky. Greenwillow Books, 1977.

Scary Stories to Tell in the Dark, collected from folklore and retold by Alvin Schwartz. J. B. Lippincott, 1981.

The Vanishing Pumpkin by Tony Johnston, illustrated by Tomie de Paola. G. P. Putnam's Sons, 1983.

The Witch of Blackbird Pond by Elizabeth Speare. Houghton Mifflin, 1958.

A Woggle of Witches by Adrienne Adams. Charles Scribner's Sons, 1971.

THE TROUBLED PILGRIM

This play, which is actually a play within a play, relays historical fact about the first Thanksgiving. In the first scene, several students discuss their Thanksgiving essay assignment, "What Thanksgiving Means to Me." One student feels there must be more to Thanksgiving than she understands. The other students leave, and she imagines the first Thanksgiving: Pilgrims and Native Americans on their way to the Thanksgiving feast try to tell a disheartened Pilgrim about the many things for which they can all be grateful. In the closing scenes, the student recognizes for the first time what the first Thanksgiving was all about and writes her essay accordingly.

WHY SHOULD CHILDREN PERFORM THIS PLAY?

This play is based upon historical accounts of the first Thanksgiving. The experiences of the first Pilgrims (in some cases, as recorded in their journals) are described by the actors as they enter and exit the stage. The intent of the play is to give children a glimpse of how bleak life had been for the Pilgrims, but that, despite all of their suffering, they found reason to give thanks. We take so much for granted these days. Imparting knowledge about the Pilgrims' struggles can help children see Thanksgiving in a new light.

Not only is the historical basis of the play one reason for performing it, but the play also stresses the role Native Americans played in that first Thanksgiving. The Pilgrims' initial fears of the natives ultimately blossomed into dependency and friendship. As such, the Pilgrims' experience demonstrated the fallacy of judging others (in this case, the Native Americans) on the basis of appearance, language, or lifestyle.

HOW SHOULD I PREPARE CHILDREN FOR PERFORMING THIS PLAY?

The special preparation suggestions for this play center around giving children a real hands-on awareness of the first Thanksgiving and the year of struggle that led up to it. Consider some of the improvisation activities suggested here, as well as the art, cooking, and writing activities, as ways to focus students on both the plot and action of the play as well as its message about thankfulness.

PERFORMING ACTIVITIES

1. **Time to Talk.** Engage the children in a discussion and improvisation of Pilgrim life. Pass out five kernels of popcorn to each child. Ask the children to look at the kernels and think about being a Pilgrim that first winter. Many mothers and fathers, sisters and brothers, and friends had died. The landscape was covered in snow. There was no heat—perhaps there was a fire when wood was available. Some lived in damp dugouts in the earth. Many lived together in the few structures that had been built. And as the winter wore on, the Pilgrims often survived on a few corn kernels a day.

Some discussion questions might be:

- How would you feel if every day, all day, you were cold, damp, and hungry?
- What would you do if your mother and father were sick and there was no medicine or food?
- How hungry would you be if you could only expect to eat a few kernels of corn every day?

Use this discussion activity as the basis for breaking into small groups and doing some improvisations of the Pilgrims' experiences. Have children spend about twenty to thirty minutes working up their scenes.

2. **Pilgrim Play.** As children read about Thanksgiving, ask them to think of some of the stories as scenes from a play. Have children work in small groups to role-play some of the more colorful Pilgrim stories. Some possible scenes are:

- As Samoset first walks into the Pilgrim settlement, the Pilgrims and their children react with fear and amazement when he speaks English.
- John Billington, a Pilgrim boy, runs off into the forest and, while Pilgrim fathers look for him, local Native Americans find him, cover him with necklaces, and bring him back to the Pilgrims.
- Squanto shows the Pilgrims how to plant corn and fertilize it with dead fish. Squanto also shows the Pilgrims which plants are safe to pick and eat.

These particular scenes will help the children understand in more detail some of the references in the play they will be performing.

▼ A Pilgrim Pantomime

From *Practical Plays*, published by GoodYearBooks. Copyright ©1993 Pamela Marx.

33

WRITING ACTIVITIES

1. **Thanksgiving Word Circles.** Have children explore the multiple meanings of words while creating ten-step word circles. Word circles are a series of short sentences that start with a key word or image, like Thanksgiving. The key word is used in a short sentence. The next sentences move to other words and then back to the key word. Some examples are:

Thanksgiving reminds me of turkey.
Turkey reminds me of gravy.
Gravy reminds me of stuffing.
Stuffing reminds me of a pillow.
A pillow reminds me of sleep.
Sleep reminds me of dreams.
Dreams remind me of wishes.
Wishes remind me of Santa Claus.
Santa Claus reminds me of Christmas.
Christmas reminds me of Thanksgiving.

Turkeys remind me of birds.
Birds remind me of feathers.
Feathers remind me of wings.
Wings remind me of airplanes.
Airplanes remind me of flying.
Flying reminds me of trips.
Trips remind me of holidays.
Holidays remind me of eating.
Eating reminds me of Thanksgiving.
Thanksgiving reminds me of turkeys.

Children should remember that for each step in the circle, they need to be able to give a plausible reason why one thing reminds them of another. It may not be self-evident, but so long as the child has a reason for the word connection, the process is successful.

Students can write this project in a circular spiral shape, if desired. Start at the middle of the circle and write out from there.

2. **Sensory Exploration Poems.** For this project, children focus on their five senses. This kind of poem has five lines and need not rhyme. Pick a noun and describe it for each sense—touch, smell, taste, sight, and hearing.

Example:

Thanksgiving feels like a brisk autumn breeze.
It smells like a hot roasting turkey.
It sounds like a crackling fire.
It tastes like pumpkin pie.
It looks like families laughing together.

3. **"Day in the Life" Stories.** Ask children to take a look at some Pilgrim resource books. Each child can then write a paragraph on a day in the life of a Pilgrim child, imagining himself or herself to be that child.

Another exercise is to have each child look at her own life. A child must think of someone or something for which she is very thankful. Then she should imagine a day in her life without that person or thing. She then writes her feelings in a paragraph or two. This exercise helps children relate their own daily experiences—their pleasures and losses—to the Pilgrims' feelings.

CROSS-CURRICULAR ACTIVITIES

1. **Pilgrim Recipes.** Cook foods similar to those the Pilgrims cooked in the first few years of the colony. Remember, sugar was scarce. Sometimes the syrup from pumpkin was used for sweetening. These recipes provide students with a better understanding of the foods the Pilgrims actually ate. Seasonings were limited, and the foods generally were more bland than the foods we eat today.

Try one of the following recipes.

BAKED PUMPKIN

Slice pumpkin into two-inch strips. Scrape the seeds and fibers from it. Place it on a greased cookie sheet and bake at 350° until tender. Serve plain or with butter and brown sugar.

▲ **Mashing Fruit**

HASTY PUDDING

Boil 4 to 5 cups of water with 1 teaspoon salt. Mix 2 cups of cornmeal with 1 cup cold water and add to the boiling water, stirring constantly. Cook over medium heat until pudding reaches desired consistency of hot cereal. Serve immediately. Makes 25 to 30 small servings. Adventurous children may want to drizzle a few drops of molasses on their cereal and mix.

APPLE-CRANBERRY CONSERVE

This fruit dish was made by early settlers when apples became available. Peel and slice about 10 large apples. Each child can chop apple slices into small pieces for cooking. Pour 3/4 cup water into saucepan or deep electric skillet and put on medium heat. Each child can then dice about 1/3 of an apple. Add the diced apples to the water as they are cut. Each child can then add a teaspoon of fresh cranberries to the mixture. Cover the mixture and mash occasionally with a potato masher. Add more water as necessary to keep from burning. If children help mash, make sure that as you remove the cover you let steam escape before children come near the pan. Add honey to taste.

2. **Pilgrim Toys.** The Pilgrims always had much work to do. Even children had chores. When they played, their toys were simple. You might want to make cornhusk dolls, which Pilgrim children used as playthings. Each doll requires at least 3 husks and 2 feet of string (sisal string looks very nice with the husks, although it tends to fray as you work.)

- Soak husks in water for one to two hours.
- Take two husks and tie the string tight with a knot around one end (about 1/2 inch from end).
- Take the long part of the husks and fold them back over the knotted area. Wrap the loose ends of the string tightly around the knotted end of husks so you form a "head" and knot again.
- Roll a third husk and slip it between the two long husks, pushing it up toward the head. This will form the arms.
- Take the ends of the string and criss-cross them over the front of the doll. Wrap them tightly under the "arms," knotting the string again. Cut off the long ends of the string.

This is a very simple doll. With adult help, primary children can do it. Third grade and up should be able to complete it without much help.

Pilgrim children also made dolls out of rags and pinecones. Can students think of ways to make a doll with natural materials? Perhaps they would like to try to make dolls out of rags.

HOW SHOULD I STAGE THIS PLAY?

This play is one of the easiest to expand or contract to meet your needs. As written, it is a Pilgrim play within a student play, with a large pantomime scene. The core of the play, however, is the "Troubled Pilgrim" scenario, which makes up the longest part of the play and was originally written as a stand-alone play. This part of the play is excellent for use with one class. Second-graders and up will probably do best with it.

If you use the "Troubled Pilgrim" scenario together with the rest of the play as written, this makes an excellent collaborative effort between two classes—one upper grade and one lower grade.

▲ **Cornhusk Dolls**

In the "Troubled Pilgrim" portion of the play, you will find parts designated as Pilgrim John/Mary and Pilgrim Thomas/Faith. You might find this confusing, but the reference is intended to assure you that either a boy or girl can play each part. In addition, since the lines of these "two" characters are crucial to the play's action, you might want to assign two students to each part and ask the two students to share the lines. In this way, if one of these crucial actors is absent from your performance, the remaining actor can pick up the lines and carry on without much trouble. Having actors double up on these two key parts provides you with a safety net in the event of illness or family conflicts.

If you choose to perform the Pilgrim play without the accompanying student scenes, you might want to end the play with a brief pantomime of the Thanksgiving feast scene together with a narrator voiceover containing elements from Student 1's final speeches. The direction the ending takes is up to you.

The narrator is not essential to the play but can help the audience understand the play's progress. This is especially true if you have difficult acoustics in your performance room or if you are concerned about your actors' projection.

▲ **Pilgrim Collars** ▼

COSTUMES

Pilgrims: Keep costuming simple. The no-sew tunics provide your basic costume. Ask Pilgrims to wear dark, long-sleeved turtleneck shirts with dark pants or dark long skirts, depending on gender. For those who do not have dark tops, use a dark no-sew tunic over long-sleeved white shirts. This has a very Pilgrim-like look. Any girl who can come up with a white apron (preferably long) should wear it. Cut collars from white butcher paper with a slit down the back. A single pin in the back holds the collars in place.

Girls should comb their hair simply, in either ponytails, buns, or straight down. Avoid huge wavy bangs and flashy curls. Ask children to think about how Pilgrim girls and women actually wore their hair.

Native Americans: These costumes require a slightly different clothing base from Pilgrim costumes. Boys should wear brown or tan pants and plain white t-shirts. Girls can wear shorts and short-sleeved t-shirts. Boys will look suitably costumed if you drape their shoulders with several three-foot strands of fringe in any autumn or natural color. Boys can also wear fringed waistbands (six to eight inches in length) cut from paper bags and marked with Native American designs. Fringe the bottom of the band and reinforce the top of the waistband with packing or masking tape. Girls should wear beige no-sew, knee-length tunics. These should be fringe cut at the bottom and marked with Native American designs just above the fringed edge.

Turkeys: The turkey actors should wear clothes in neutral colors and beige tunics. The tunics can be cut longer in back and marked with felt markers to look like tail feathers. Cut wings out of grocery bags. The bags should be cut into strips about ten inches wide and twenty-four inches long. Use two strips of paper bag for each wing. Staple them together and mark them with felt pens to look like feathered wings. The actors will hold the undersides of the wings in their hands to keep them in place.

SCENERY

Your scenery depends on how much help and space you have available. If you choose to do without scenery, the play will not be hurt. If you choose to use scenery and you are doing the full play with all scenes, the scenery must be moveable.

Consider doing without scenery for the first student scene. For the Pilgrim scenery, use free-standing trees, perhaps painted on tagboard and attached to chairs, or cut out of paper and pinned to a curtain. For the last student scene, the child can be dressed in a robe as though ready for bed. She can be sitting at her desk or simply sitting in a chair and pantomiming completion of her school paper.

▲ **Turkey Costume and Wing**

THE TROUBLED PILGRIM STUDENT SCRIPT

PLAYERS

Narrator

Student 1 (Jenny)

Student 2

Student 3

Student 4

Pilgrim Women (1 to 3)

Assorted Pilgrim Women and Children

Pilgrim John/Mary (depending on
    gender of actor)

Pilgrim Thomas/Faith (depending on gender of actor)

Speaking Pilgrims (1 to 19)

Squanto

Assorted Native Americans and
    Pilgrims to engage in
    pantomime activities

Pilgrim Hunter

Turkeys

Native American Dancers

Note: Since the Pilgrims John/Mary and Thomas/Faith parts are essential to this play, each part can be shared by two people. Two are disheartened; two are optimistic. In this way, if someone has to miss a performance, another actor can easily step into the absentee's shoes.

PROPS

First Student Scene: books, notebooks, pencils, bookbags, and knapsacks

Pilgrim Scenes: baskets, pots, unsliced and unwrapped bread loaves, large pot, wooden spoons, Indian corn, squash, pumpkins, several pieces of firewood, pole with shape of tagboard deer stapled or tied to it, picnic benches, toy rifle (optional), drum

Last Student Scene: desk or chair, paper, pencils

Curtain rises.

Scene 1

Students standing around the schoolyard after school, talking about homework. Some knapsacks and notebooks are on the ground.

Student 1

Why do we have to write a paper on Thanksgiving, anyway?

Student 2

Oh, stop complaining. It's no big deal. Thanksgiving is for giving thanks.

Student 3

Yeah, we do it every year. You write that you're thankful for your family, your home, your food.

Student 4 (in a sarcastic manner)

Yes, I'm thankful, but not much.

Student 1

I don't know. I don't think I really understand what the Pilgrims were all about.

Student 2 (picking up knapsack)

Well, that's not my problem. I gotta go.

Student 3

Yeah, me too. See you later.

Student 4 (smugly)

I'm going to go home and whip that paper out in nothing flat. See you.

Student 1

See you. *(packs up, walks a step or two toward the audience, then stops to think)*
I wonder . . .

Lights fade or curtain falls.

Curtain rises.

Scene 2

A wooded area. If space allows, at some remote part of the staging area, Pilgrim women pantomime cooking.

If you decide to use two "discouraged" Pilgrims instead of one, adjust the narrator text accordingly so that the Narrator refers to "two Pilgrims" who remain discouraged, not one. Also, if a boy plays the character of Student 1, adjust the Narrator text to use an appropriate boy's name, such as John.

Narrator

Jenny tried to imagine that first Thanksgiving celebration so long ago. In her mind, she saw the Pilgrims preparing for the feast. The women hurried with their cooking and tended the children. But in the midst of the festivities, one Pilgrim remained discouraged. That Pilgrim did not feel very thankful.

Pilgrim Woman 1 (enters with pot on way to feast)

We have much cooking to do to prepare for the feast.

Pilgrim Woman 2 (carrying cooking supplies or food)

Yes, there will be so many to feed.

Pilgrim Woman 3 (enters with pot on way to feast—she calls over her shoulder)

Hurry and bring the children.

Here assorted Pilgrim Women and Children enter on the way to the feast. (Kindergarten children enjoy playing the children in this walk-on part. While the kindergarten children sit momentarily on stage, older primary children who are still unable to carry crucial lines can tell them to "hurry, hurry" while shaking fingers at them.) Pilgrim Women and Children exit.

When the stage is empty, one or two Turkeys jump out on stage and flee from the Pilgrim Hunter, who then jumps out on stage. This is intended as comic relief. Have Turkeys stop at intervals, look over their shoulders and flail their "wings" in fear.

Turkeys exit with Pilgrim Hunter chasing them.

Enter Pilgrim John/Mary. He/she stops on stage to the side of center. Pilgrim John/Mary waves to approaching Pilgrim.

Enter Pilgrim Thomas/Faith.

Note: The lines for John/Mary and Thomas/Faith are for example only. Actors can adjust them and find their own words to say. The concepts underlying the lines are repetitious and children can give themselves simple lines based on the repeating themes.

Pilgrim John/Mary

Say, friend, why such a sad face? Today is the day of our thanksgiving feast.

Pilgrim Thomas/Faith

Bah, what do we have to be thankful for? *(angrily)* We had such a bad winter last year. We lost so many loved ones. And for what? *(pauses) You* go to the feast. I don't feel very thankful.

Pilgrim John/Mary

Oh, friend, we must talk about this. You know we came to this new land and struggled to get here so that we could have the freedom to believe and do what we think is right.

Pilgrim Thomas/Faith

Yes, I know, but we have suffered so much. Was it worth it?

Pilgrim John/Mary

We must talk more about this.

Narrator

As the Pilgrims talked, other Pilgrims passed on their way to the feast. They were very joyful and very thankful. These Pilgrims told how they were thankful for their new homes and for their new freedom.

Several Pilgrims pass by. They carry baskets and squash for the feast.

Pilgrim John/Mary

Perhaps these good neighbors coming down the path can help us.

Pilgrim Thomas/Faith

Humph.

Pilgrim John/Mary (hailing the passersby)

Hello, good neighbors.

Passing Pilgrims

Hello, friends.

Pilgrim John/Mary

Pilgrim Thomas here is discouraged. Can you tell him what you are thankful for this fine day?

From *Practical Plays*, published by GoodYearBooks. Copyright ©1993 Pamela Marx.

Pilgrim 1

Oh, yes, we have so much to be thankful for. We have our homes to keep us warm.

Pilgrim 2

Remember when we first came? We had only one house—our common house.

Pilgrim 3

Yes, and some of us lived in dugouts in the earth that we covered with sod. The winds blew cold that winter.

Pilgrim 4

Well, now we have many good houses standing strong and safe.

Pilgrim 5

We have been through much sickness and cold and hunger, but we have learned so many things. This winter we will be much better prepared.

Pilgrim 6

Yes, and we can live in our new homes, free to believe and do what we know is right.

Pilgrim 7

We are making good progress in this new land. We hope you will join in the thanksgiving feast.

Passing Pilgrims

Goodbye, good friends. *(They leave, talking and chatting.)* See you at the feast.

Pilgrim John/Mary

Goodbye. Well, Pilgrim Thomas, what do you say now?

Pilgrim Thomas/Faith

Oh, I don't know. I'm not sure that is enough. After all we've been through . . .

Narrator

As the Pilgrims talked, more Pilgrims passed by on their way to the feast. They were feeling very thankful. They were especially thankful for their new friends, Squanto and the Wampanoags.

More Pilgrims enter, together with Squanto and Native American guests, on their way to the feast.

Pilgrim John/Mary

Perhaps these neighbors can help us more. *(calling to the passing Pilgrims and Native Americans)* Friends, can you tell us what you are thankful for this fine day?

Pilgrim 8

Oh yes. When we came here, this was a cold land, and we had no friends.

Pilgrim 9

But now we know Squanto and the Wampanoags and they are good friends. At first we feared them, but now we are thankful for their help and friendship.

Pilgrim 10

Our friend Squanto here *(points to Squanto)* has taught us many things. Tell them, Squanto.

Squanto

I showed you how to grow corn—to dig the hole, to fill it with tiny fish to feed the soil and then to plant the seed. And our planting together has done well this year.

Pilgrim 11 (to Squanto and Pilgrim Thomas)

Squanto, you also taught us which foods of the forest we could eat, how to prepare them and how to dry them for the winter.

Pilgrim 12

Yes, and you taught us how to hunt deer and turkeys and geese. Now we have much to eat.

Squanto or Other Native American

And the Wampanoags have been your friends, too. Remember when the young Billington boy wandered into the forest and was lost?

Pilgrim 13

Yes, I remember. The great Massasoit, chief of the Wampanoag tribe, signaled us that the boy had been found. They decorated the boy with beads and carried him back to our settlement.

Pilgrim 8

Yes, we have good friends in this new land. We have much to be thankful for.

Passing Pilgrims and Native Americans (speaking all together as they leave)

Goodbye. Goodbye. See you at the feast.

Pilgrims and Native Americans exit toward the feast.

Pilgrim John/Mary

Thank you, friends. See you later.

Pilgrim Thomas/Faith

Pilgrim John, I am beginning to see what you mean. Still, I can't help but think of all the suffering, of all the friends and family members who are no longer with us.

Pilgrim John/Mary

I know, but they came to America because they believed it was important to be free. They wanted to come. Look, here are more neighbors. Let's get their thoughts. *(waves to passing Pilgrims)*

Narrator

The discouraged Pilgrim began to understand how the other Pilgrims felt. As more Pilgrims passed, they told how grateful they were for the good harvest they had.

Pilgrims enter on their way to the feast.

Pilgrim John/Mary

Hey, neighbors. Can you tell us what you are thankful for today?

Pilgrim 14

We'd be glad to. We have so much to be thankful for.

Pilgrim 15

We certainly do. Just last winter we had so little food that we lived on only a few kernels of corn a day. We hardly made it through the winter. Some of us didn't.

Pilgrim 16

But look at our crops this year. It is truly a bountiful harvest. We planted corn and it grew tall.

Pilgrim 17

And the woods are full of many berries and fruits. There are plums, gooseberries, and cherries.

Pilgrim 18

And the forests are full of game, which our friend Squanto has taught us to hunt.

Pilgrim 19

And don't forget the sea. It is full of fish and clams and lobsters and oysters.

Pilgrim 14

You see, there is so much to be thankful for today, it is hard to know where to begin.

Pilgrim John/Mary

Thank you, good neighbors. We will see you at the feast.

Passing Pilgrims exit.

Pilgrim John/Mary

Indeed, there is much to be thankful for. Do you agree now, Pilgrim Thomas?

Pilgrim Thomas/Faith

Yes, yes. You were right, Pilgrim John. It is still true that we have suffered much. We have lost loved ones. We have been cold and hungry. But we have learned many things and we will go on.

Pilgrim John/Mary

Yes, we are in a new world with all its possibilities. And we have our freedom.

Pilgrim Thomas/Faith

We have much to be thankful for. May I join you at the feast?

Pilgrim John/Mary

Most certainly.

Pilgrims John/Mary and Thomas/Faith exit toward the feast.

Turkeys reenter, fleeing the Pilgrim Hunter. He follows and they exit. Turkeys should look over their shoulders and flap wings in fright.

Lights fade/curtain falls.

If pantomimed feast area is located in front of the curtain, and if there are actors located in these areas, all of these actors freeze.

Narrator

And so the discouraged Pilgrim saw the Pilgrims' struggles in a new light. The Pilgrim headed toward the feast with a new feeling of happiness and thankfulness. As Jenny imagined these Pilgrims, she began to understand for the first time what that first Thanksgiving was all about.

Curtain rises.

Scene 3

Schoolyard scene with Student 1 standing alone daydreaming in the same position she held at the end of Scene 1.

Student 1 (wondering aloud to herself)

Yes, I can see now how the Pilgrims must have felt that first Thanksgiving. It helps me to see better all the things that I have, that I take for granted. *(packing up school books and starting to leave)* Maybe for the first time this year I really understand what Thanksgiving means.

Student 1 exits.

Lights fade/curtain falls.

Curtain rises.

Scene 4

Lights on Student 1 at home writing her Thanksgiving paper.

Student 1

Let's see. I've got to finish this paper. Now where was I?
Oh, yes . . .

She puts her pen down, holds up the paper and reads aloud the end of it. If the Pilgrim feast scene is located behind a curtain, curtain opens.

Student 1

And so the Pilgrims celebrated and gave thanks for three days. The Native Americans brought game. The women cooked. The men played games of skill. It was a joyful scene.

Student 1 freezes while action begins in pantomime scene.

In the pantomime scene, the Pilgrims are seen at their first Thanksgiving feast. Women are cooking. Pilgrims and the Native Americans who passed by Pilgrims John/Mary and Thomas/Faith are standing around chatting. Several Native Americans arrive carrying slain deer (made from posterboard) on poles held on their shoulders or carrying burlap bags (props). Some Pilgrims and Native Americans are playing test-of-skill games (such as who can jump highest).

The Native American Dancers enter and do a short dance to drumming by other Native Americans. When the dancers finish, the Pilgrim Hunter enters proudly with the captured turkeys behind him gobbling woefully. He presents the captured turkeys to the Pilgrim Women.

The pantomime scene freezes while Student 1 continues.

Student 1

Yes, the Pilgrims had much to be thankful for. They had homes and friends and food. And they had their freedom. These are the same things we think of at Thanksgiving today. This is what Thanksgiving is all about. The End.

Student 1 pauses and tilts head. She is happy with her work.

Student 1

Yeah. *(She smiles.)* I like it. *(pause)* And happy Thanksgiving to us all.

Fade to final curtain.

Curtain falls.

THE END

SUGGESTED READINGS

The First Thanksgiving Feast by Joan Anderson. Clarion Books, 1984.

It's Thanksgiving by Jack Prelutsky. Greenwillow Books, 1982.

The Landing of the Pilgrims by James Daugherty. Random House, 1950.

Oh, What a Thanksgiving by Steven Kroll. Scholastic, 1988.

Sarah Morton's Day by Kate Waters. Scholastic, 1989.

Squanto, First Friend to the Pilgrims by Cathy East Dubowski. Dell, 1990.

The Thanksgiving Story by Alice Dalgliesh. Charles Scribner's Sons, 1954.

SUGGESTED SONGS

Have the children sing one or more of these songs before or after the play performance.

"Come, Ye Thankful People Come," a traditional Thanksgiving hymn (contains religious references)

"Gather in the Harvest," a Finnish folk song

"Over the River and Through the Woods" by Lydia Maria Child

"Simple Gifts," a Shaker folk song arranged by Aaron Copeland

"This Land Is Your Land" by Woody Guthrie

"We Gather Together," a traditional Thanksgiving hymn (contains religious references)

OLD FROST'S WINTER ADVENTURE

Old Frost's Winter Adventure

A Winter Holiday Play

This play explores winter festivals around the world and is suitable for a winter or Christmas program. In the play, Old Frost travels the world with his/her icy helpers. As they travel, they happen upon a variety of winter festivals. They watch the holiday scenes unfold before their eyes until the icy winds carry them away to a different country where they view a different holiday tradition.

WHY SHOULD CHILDREN PERFORM THIS PLAY?

This play dovetails nicely with any curriculum on world cultures, world geography, or world events. Since it is intended for use as a winter holiday program, it explores different Christmas practices as well as Hanukkah and Chinese New Year celebrations. If the countries covered by the play are not suitable, you could substitute short vignettes reflecting practices from countries you would like to cover. The countries used here were chosen, at least in part, because well-known songs identified with the countries could be incorporated into the performance. Since these songs are already familiar to many children, they are easy for children to learn and perform.

The play can be an eye-opener for children. As they work on the play, they begin to realize that holiday customs and practices that they take for granted had their origins outside the United States. This is a valuable insight for children and should help them develop an overall appreciation of the peoples and customs of the countries of our world.

Another reason to perform this play is that, depending upon how you decide to stage it, it can combine recitation, singing, and dancing. As with the Halloween play, this gives children an opportunity to perform in several media through one vehicle.

HOW SHOULD I PREPARE CHILDREN FOR PERFORMING THIS PLAY?

One basic way to prepare children to perform this play is to study one of many available curricula on Christmas celebrations around the world. This helps children better understand the full meaning of the holiday celebrations they reenact in the play. Even if you don't study Christmas around the world in your class, you'll find brief background information on each of the play's winter festivals in this chapter. This information will enable you to teach a short multicultural holiday course

without purchasing additional materials. Also included are suggested activities for each winter festival represented in the play.

BACKGROUND INFORMATION ON WINTER FESTIVALS

HANUKKAH

Hanukkah is the eight-day Jewish festival of lights that falls sometime in December each year. It is celebrated by Jews the world over. The festival celebrates the victory of Judah and the Maccabees over the huge army of the Greek king Antiochus, who had previously gained control over the Jews. After a long war, the Jews won.

A legend relating to the victory relates to the lighting of the temple lamp. After the victory, the Jews returned to their temple to find it badly vandalized. They cleaned and repaired it and prepared to light the temple lamp. To light the holy lamp, they needed oil that had been specially made and blessed. They found only enough oil to burn for a short time. Miraculously, the oil burned for eight days until new oil had been made and blessed. This story tells of the miracle of Hanukkah.

The main symbols of the holiday are the Hanukkah *menorah* and the *dreidel*. The Hanukkah menorah is a candle holder that holds nine candles—one for each night of Hanukkah, and the *shamash*, or helper candle, which is used to light the others. The dreidel is a four-sided top. At Hanukkah, children play a traditional holiday game with the dreidel. Symbols on each side of the top (*shin*, *hay*, *nun*, and *gimmel*) tell players whether they lose or keep their goodies, called *gelt*. Gold-covered candy coins or nuts are the gelt for which the players play.

The traditional Hanukkah dish is potato pancakes, called *latkes*. They are served with sour cream or applesauce.

CHRISTMAS

German Christmas. German settlers brought to America the holiday customs of the Christmas tree, the Advent wreath, the Advent calendar, and some favorite carols. Many myths surround the creation of the first Christmas tree. Some say Martin Luther, the famous Protestant reformer, cut the first tree. He looked up through the forest branches one night to see the stars sparkling through the trees. He was so impressed by the sight that he cut down a tree, took it home, and filled it with lighted candles.

Others say the tradition derives from a blending of early German customs. One was a celebration of the story of Adam and Eve in which apples were hung on evergreen trees. This celebration was followed by Christmas during which candelabra-type structures called *lightstocks* were lit. Gradually, the two customs may have merged, resulting in a decorated and candlelit evergreen tree.

One German custom that involves the Christmas tree is special to children. In some households, a pickle is the last decoration placed on the tree on Christmas Eve. It is hidden among the decorations. The first child to find the pickle on the tree gets a special surprise.

Several other customs of German origin relate to Advent. Advent is the four-Sunday period that precedes Christmas Day. For those who celebrate the religious significance of Christmas, it is a time for thoughtful introspection about the meaning of Christmas Day as well as a time to prepare oneself for the Christmas Day celebration of Jesus' birth. As part of this Advent period, the use of Advent calendars and Advent wreaths developed.

The Advent calendar started as a picture with 24 doors numbered 1 to 24. Each day during December the door corresponding to that day in December was opened to reveal a tiny picture. The door for day 24 usually opened on a picture of a manger scene. In modern versions of the Advent calendar, the doors often hide candy or chocolate treats.

The Advent wreath is a wreath or other holder that sits on a table with four candles in it—one for each of the four Sundays preceding Christmas. On each Sunday of this four-week period called Advent, the candles are lighted—one for the first Sunday, two for the second Sunday, and so on.

English Christmas. Many long-standing "American" Christmas traditions came to the United States via England. The custom of sending Christmas cards began in England in the mid-1800s. Mince pies are English confections. Draping doorways and windows with greenery (the holly and the ivy) is a long-standing tradition. Mistletoe, with its pale green leaves and eerie white berries, was thought to possess mystic powers by ancient people. Over time, its use became a source of holiday antics as the tradition of kissing under the mistletoe developed. (Perhaps this custom symbolizes the peace and love of the season.) In addition, many famous Christmas carols have English origins.

Mexican Christmas. In Mexico, an important holiday tradition begins nine days before Christmas. It is called *Las Posadas*, and it is largely steeped in the country's Roman Catholic traditions. Each night of *Las Posadas*, Mary's and Joseph's journey to the inn is reenacted. Mary and Joseph travel from door to door in a neighborhood or room to room in a house. At each door, they are sent away until, at the last door, the travellers are asked in to view a manger scene and to enjoy a piñata party.

The focal point of the *Las Posadas* piñata party is the striking and breaking of the piñata. A piñata is a hollow papier-mâché creation that is covered with brightly colored tissue and crêpe paper. The structure may be an animal, a person, a star, or any fanciful creature. A tiny door cut into the papier-mâché allows the piñata to be filled with candies and treats. At the party, children take turns trying to break the piñata, which is hung from a tree or from the ceiling, if the party is indoors. Each child is blindfolded and given a stick. He or she tries to break the piñata as it sways in the air. When the piñata finally breaks, children run to pick up as much candy as they can as fast as they can.

An interesting holiday fact is that the poinsettia comes from Mexico. Now a traditional Christmas plant in the United States, it was brought to this country in the mid-1800s by America's first ambassador to Mexico, Joel Poinsett. The flower was named after him. The red "petals" are really the plant's leaves and the flowers are the tiny yellow buds at the center of the red leaves.

CHINESE NEW YEAR

The new year is a very important holiday in China. It usually falls somewhere between mid-January and mid-February. It is a multi-day festival. On the third day of the festival, a great dragon parade is held. In accordance with long-standing custom, people beat pots and pans and make loud noises with noisemakers to scare away evil from the new year.

Children look forward to gifts of money which are wrapped in red and placed on a money tree. The color red is important to the holiday and signifies good luck.

PERFORMING ACTIVITIES

The following activities are designed to give children a hands-on understanding of the games, dances, and customs they will reenact in the play.

▲ nun   gimmel

▲ hey   shin

1. **Learn to Play Dreidel.** To make a simple dreidel, cut a 2-inch square of tagboard or posterboard. On each side of the square, write one of the four Hebrew letters—shin, hey, nun, and gimmel.

   Hole-punch a hole in the center of the square and insert a sharpened pencil stub (pencil should be about three to four inches long). Push the square up the pencil so that it is between 1 inch and 1-1/4 inch from the pointed end of the pencil. Twist the top of the pencil to spin the dreidel.

   You need six people to play dreidel. Give everyone an equal number of gelt pieces, such as pennies, nuts, or wrapped candies. Each player then puts one piece of gelt into the "pot." Players take turns spinning the dreidel. If it lands shin side up, the player who spun gives one piece of gelt to the pot. If it lands hay side up, that player gets to take half of the gelt from the pot. If it lands gimmel side up, the player takes all the coins from the pot. If it lands nun side up, the player gets nothing. When the pot empties out after a gimmel, each player puts one piece of gelt back in the pot and the game goes on. The winner is the player at the end of play with the most gelt.

2. **Dance the _Hora_.** The _hora_ is a traditional Jewish dance. The steps are:

   - Step to the right with the right foot.
   - Step to the right with the left foot crossing in front of the right foot.
   - Step to the right with the right foot and then jump on the right foot.
   - Step on the left foot and then jump on the left foot.
   - Repeat the sequence.

   If the actual _hora_ is too difficult for children to learn, children can do a simpler dance here using just the grapevine step. The grapevine step is a basic folk dance step: right foot crosses over in front of left foot; step left one step with left foot; right foot crosses behind left foot, step left one step with left foot, repeat.

▲ **Playing Dreidel**

From _Practical Plays_, published by GoodYearBooks. Copyright ©1993 Pamela Marx.

3. **Mime a Holiday Scene.** Through pantomime, children explore how to communicate ideas and actions without words. Have children work in small groups to pantomime some holiday scenes about some of the Christmas customs covered in the play. Remind them that even for pantomime they need to determine who the characters are and what they are doing. Also, since they cannot use words to convey the action, their movements must be exaggerated and "large."

Some Christmas customs for pantomime are:

• Decorating the Christmas tree. Children explore picking out ornaments, sorting through boxes, stringing popcorn and cranberries, reaching high and low on the tree to place decorations, shooshing children off to bed, and hiding the pickle on the tree.

• Reenacting a Christmas tree legend. Children can reenact the legend of Martin Luther thinking of the first Christmas tree, cutting it, carrying it home, placing candles on it, and lighting them.

• Decorating the house with garlands. Children "deck the hall" with holly, ivy, and evergreens. They pretend to decorate windows, lights, mantles, and doorways. As part of the exercise, they can pretend to measure the places to be decorated and look over the garland for just the right piece.

• Sneaking a peek at presents. Children can explore wrapping gifts, placing them under the tree, sneaking a look at presents others have wrapped, and shaking presents to find out what treasures they hold.

• Participating in a piñata party. Children explore filling a piñata, hanging it up, making it move up and down, lining up to break it, swinging at it, and racing after candy and treats when the piñata breaks.

• Creating a *Las Posadas* procession. Children explore parading wayfarers asking for room, being turned down and sent on their way, knocking at more doors, and finally being invited in and given a place to rest.

4. *La Raspa.* The music for this well-known Mexican folk dance is readily available. The dance is performed with partners. It is done as follows:

• Partners face each other. One partner puts the left heel forward on the floor, then the right heel forward on the floor, then the left heel forward on the floor, in time with the music.

• The dancer repeats this action once, but this time he or she starts with the right foot, then repeats the entire six-step sequence.

- The other partner does the same steps simultaneously.
- Partners then join right arms at the elbow and turn in a circle to the music for about eight counts, clap, and then change arms and reverse direction.

If you use this dance in the play, repeat the entire sequence twice.

5. **New Year Noisemaking.** Have children use percussion instruments or hand-made noisemakers such as rattles to create rhythm bands. Have groups practice the rhythms to different songs and dances for the play. Have a group play the rhythm part of a song, and see if the rest of the class can identify the song. This is a good exercise for reinforcing the rhythm and beat of both song and dance segments from the play.

Some of the songs in the play lend themselves well to limited percussion accompaniment. Perhaps you want to use this activity as a starting place for deciding which students will provide such accompaniment during the play. Some percussion ideas are maracas for "Feliz Navidad" and bells for "Jingle Bells" and "Deck the Halls."

WRITING ACTIVITIES

1. **Create a Holiday.** The winter holiday play is about celebrations that occur around the world. Have children create their own holiday. It could be structured something like this:

If I could make up my own holiday, it would celebrate _____. (child fills in the subject of the celebration, such as sunshine, trees, me, or summer vacation)

I would dance like . . .
I would sing like . . .
I would eat . . .
I would wear . . .

Example:

On my holiday, I would celebrate the first day of summer.
I would dance like an ocean wave on the shore.
I would sing around a campfire.
I would eat s'mores all night long.
I would wear my bathing suit so I could swim any time I wanted.

2. **A Sensory Exploration Poem.** (This activity is described in some detail in the Writing Activities section of Chapter 2.) Children can either choose their own winter holiday to write about, or you can assign the project to reflect a specific holiday, such as New Year.

3. **Acrostics.** Holidays that children know well are good opportunities for doing acrostics. Simply using holiday names should provide adequate creative opportunity.

Example:

C is for candles that flicker and flame.
H is for holly that "decks the hall."
R is for rice pudding, a Scandinavian holiday treat.
I is for icicles after a snowfall.
S is for snowmen that the children build.
T is for trees of noble, fir, and pine.
M is for mince pie and other tasty treats.
A is for angels sitting atop the trees.
S is for stars that light the Christmas sky.

4. **New Year's Scrolls.** Give the children long sheets of white paper. Ask them to write new year's greetings and wishes that they want to give to others. Tell them to be creative and colorful. This exercise is reminiscent of the Chinese new year practice of decorating homes with beautiful scrolls containing new year wishes. Have children write their greetings in red or orange marker or crayon and paint designs. Chinese characters provide good design decoration.

Example:

In your new year,
May you be healthy.
May you have many friends.
May you have all the toys you want.
May you get good grades in school.

Perhaps children can draw names and create their scrolls to send wishes to their partners. An alternative scroll project would be to have children write their new year wishes as wishes to the world.

Example:

In the new year, I wish for the world many things.
May all the people of the world be fed.
May there be no war.
May there be clean air to breathe.
May there be love between all the creatures on earth.

5. **Short Essays on Favorite Holiday Memories or Traditions.** If you ask children to explore a tradition, you have created an opportunity for them to talk about traditions, customs, and legends, from a personal perspective and how customs are created within a family and passed down from parent to child. In an essay, each child should identify the holiday, his or her age at the time of the event described, who was involved, why it was memorable, and if the holiday event will be repeated from year to year.

CROSS-CURRICULAR ACTIVITIES

1. **Hanukkah Puzzle.** Have children draw a menorah on a plain sheet of paper (or make a sample and copy it for each child). Have them color the picture, and then glue it to construction paper of the same size. Using a ruler and pencil, the child can draw horizontal lines at one- or two-inch intervals down the page. Cut along these lines, and you have a complete puzzle.

The puzzle cuts can be of any shape, of course, and older children may want to make up their own, cutting the puzzle into no more than nine pieces.

▲ **A Hanukkah Puzzle**

2. **Potato Latkes.** Recipes abound for making potato pancakes. Grated potatoes, eggs, and flour are mixed together and fried. A sample recipe is:

3 large potatoes
1 medium onion
4 tablespoons flour
1 egg
1/4 teaspoon salt
Few shakes of pepper
Vegetable oil for frying

- Clean potatoes and cut out any dark spots. Grate them into a bowl. (To do this activity easily in a group setting, it really helps to have a food processor; otherwise you might want to have the potatoes and onions grated in advance.)
- Peel outer skin from the onion and grate the onion into the bowl. If possible, press out any excess liquid from mixture.
- Add flour and mix. Beat egg slightly and add to mixture. Season with salt and pepper.
- Pour about 4 tablespoons of oil into a frying pan (replenish as necessary during frying process). Oil should be about one-quarter inch deep. Heat over high heat.
- When oil is heated, fry latkes by dropping tablespoonfuls of mixture into the pan. Flatten them with a wooden spoon or spatula and fry both sides until medium brown. Drain on paper towels.

Making latkes this way is authentic, but quite a bit of work. They cook up a little like pancakes made of hash brown potatoes. A simpler, but still tasty, way to make latkes is to use one of the boxed latke mixes. These mixes are available in the specialty food section of most markets around Hanukkah.

3. **Advent Calendar Bulletin Board.** Cut a large Christmas tree shape for the bulletin board. Then cut a number of 2- to 3-inch construction-paper circles in colors of your choice. Each child gets two circles. On one circle the child draws with pencil, markers, or crayons a tiny holiday scene. It can be a scene from any winter festival or a holiday symbol.

Each child is then given a number from 1 through 24. On the second circle, he or she writes that number in thick felt marker. The first picture circle is glued to the tree. The numbered circle is stapled on the top of the picture circle so that it can be pulled off as the days pass. If you have more than 24 children, have the

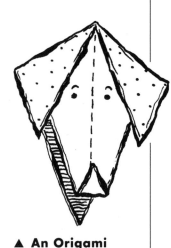

▲ **An Origami Ornament**

remaining children write holiday messages on their cover circles — Merry Christmas, Feliz Navidad (Spanish), Buon Natale (Italian), Joyeux Noel (French), or Frolich Kerstfeest (Dutch).

To ensure the multicultural aspects of the bulletin board, you might also cut out a menorah shape (Hanukkah) and a dragon shape (Chinese New Year) to adorn part of the board. Title the board "Winter Festivals Around the World."

4. **Multicultural Tree Ornaments.** Have children make ornaments of many cultures to decorate the classroom, or give as presents to parents. Some possibilities are:

- Check your local library for books on simple origami. Choose one or two designs. Using a piece of construction paper about 5 or 6 inches square, demonstrate, step by step, how a particular item is made. Then have the children all fold their projects one fold at a time. Hold the paper up and show them what you are doing each step of the way. Wait after each step so that all the children are with you. Most simple designs have no more than six folds. Punch a hole at the top of the completed piece and hang with yarn or ribbon.

- Make an Ojo de Dios, or "eye of God." This is a traditional craft from Mexico that is supposed to ward off evil and bring good luck. To make this project, you will need two popsicle sticks (or small wooden barbeque skewers with the pointed ends cut off) and bright-colored yarn. Lay the two sticks on top of each other perpendicularly. Starting with an 18-inch piece of yarn, cross the yarn in an "x" at the center of the two sticks so that they are held together at right angles from one another. Take the remaining length of yarn and begin wrapping it around each stick (over and around each stick), one stick at a time, moving from the center out. As you wrap the yarn, place each new wrap next to the yarn from the last wrap so that the "eye" grows. You can change yarn colors as you like by simply cutting the yarn you are working with and tying on a new color.

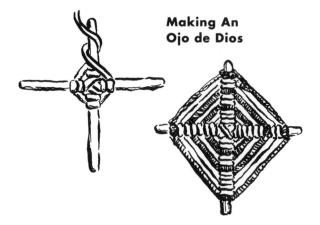

Making An Ojo de Dios

From *Practical Plays*, published by GoodYearBooks. Copyright ©1993 Pamela Marx.

5. **No-Bake Fruitcake.** Many children have never tried fruitcake, or, if they have, they have decided that they do not like it. This is a fruitcake-like confection that requires no baking and seems to be palatable to children. It introduces them to a holiday food tradition from England.

1 pound mini-marshmallows	8 ounces chopped candied red cherries
1 pound butter	8 ounces chopped dried pineapple
4 tablespoons brown sugar	1 pound chopped dates
1-1/2 teaspoons vanilla	1 pound diced walnuts or pecans
1 16-ounce box of graham crackers, finely crushed	

- Crush the graham crackers with a roller.
- Melt the first four ingredients slowly over medium heat. Pour this mixture over fruits and nuts, and mix well.
- Drop this mixture by large spoonfuls into another bowl that contains crushed graham crackers. Work as much of the graham crackers as possible into the marshmallow fruit mixture.
- Take the mixture and roll it into rolls two inches in diameter.
- Roll in foil and refrigerate overnight.
- Unwrap the rolls and cut them into quarter-inch slices. You can place several slices on a holiday plate and use it as a holiday gift to parents.

6. **Mini-piñatas.** Use two small paper cups (5 ounce), glue, yarn, a pencil, and tissue paper squares (one inch square) to make these small piñatas.

- Before you begin, thread a loop of yarn with a knot at one end through a hole in the bottom of one cup. The loop should be on the outside and the knot on the inside. Put a dot of glue on the knot and hole to secure.
- Then cover the entire exterior surface of each cup with tissue paper. Use the eraser end of the pencil to do this. Place the center of each tissue square on the eraser and push the remainder of the paper up the sides of the pencil.
- Dip the eraser end of the pencil, which is covered with tissue paper, lightly in white glue and place it on the cup. The tissue will stick to the cup and you can do another tissue square. Repeat until cups are covered.

When dry, drop some small candies into one cup, put glue on the lip edges of each cup, and glue the piñata together. While this project is a little time-consuming, it is very pretty when complete. If you use red, white, and green tissue, the tiny piñata has both Christmas colors and the colors of the Mexican

**▲ Make a
New Year
Dragon Toy**

flag. These mini-piñatas make good gifts for parents, siblings, or pen-pals and can also be used as tree ornaments.

7. **New Year Dragons.** Give each child a nine- to twelve-inch diameter circle of posterboard or a stiff paper plate. Using scraps of construction paper, feathers, and fabric, have children create a dragon face on the circle. It should have large eyes and a large mouth. Have children look at pictures of new year dragons in books before they begin. Attach 24-inch crêpe-paper streamers to six points of the circle. For colors, use primarily red, yellow/gold, orange, and black. Use masking tape to tape the dragon to a dowel made of rolled posterboard or a cardboard stick from a dry-cleaning hanger. As the dragon is waved through the air, the streamers fly. These crafts can be used in the play, if desired.

8. **New Year's Noisemaker.** Excellent noisemakers can be made from aluminum soda cans.

- Remove the pop top from the can. Tell children to be careful as they do this and remind them to keep their fingers out of the can as the drinking hole can be sharp.
- Children cover the outsides of their cans using an appropriately sized strip of construction paper, which they have colored or decorated as desired.
- Fill each can one-quarter to one-half inch full with beans, rice, barley, sand, aquarium gravel, or pop tops.
- Tape the hole shut with masking tape. Three small pieces usually does the trick.
- Then glue a circle of colored construction paper, which is the diameter of the top of the can, over the end of the taped hole.

These noisemakers sound great and last a long time. Another way to make noisemakers is to use toilet paper rolls. These are not as loud as the "can" noisemakers.

- Push each side of the roll toward the middle so that one end of the roll is largely closed. Tape the end shut.
- Then take a handful of dry beans, raw rice, or other small noisy objects and place them in the tube.
- Push the other end of the tube closed, and tape that end closed.

- Cut a twelve-inch square of tissue paper and three 24-inch crêpe-paper streamers. Lay the tissue paper flat and place the streamers flat on top of the tissue paper. (The ends of the streamers will extend six inches on either side of the tissue.)
- Place the closed tube at one end of the tissue and roll the tissue and streamers around the tube. Tie the tissue at each end of the tube with ribbon or yarn. The streamers hang out from either end to give a festive look as children shake the noisemakers. These can also be used in the play.

HOW SHOULD I STAGE THIS PLAY?

This particular play can be staged in any of several ways. First, if you have two classes participating, one class can act as chorus throughout the entire play and the other class can provide the actors for each scene. Using two classes in this way allows for the action part of the play to be staged in a simple entry and exit manner. Each group of actors enters, performs, and exits, leaving the stage empty except for Old Frost and the helpers.

If children are acting both as actors and chorus, you will need to arrange access to and from the staging area so that children always return to a location from which they can sing. This method helps increase the number of children available at all times to sing the songs. Do this by placing the chorus at each side of the stage and grouping actors together within the chorus so that each acting group can move to and from the chorus without having to crawl over other children.

Another way to stage the play is for the characters of Old Frost and Helpers to line up at the front of the staging area between scenes. Instead of whirling about the stage as described in the play directions, they could extend their arms between each other and sway as they give their lines. In this way these actors draw attention away from the actor entrances and exits that may take place behind them.

Finally, it is also possible to do a version of this play as a five-to six-minute mini-play using the portions of the play relating to England, Germany, Mexico, and America. In this shortened version, Old Frost becomes Santa and the play is called "Santa's Busy Night." It is a good Christmas performance piece for a 30- to 40-child chorus or for a single class as part of a larger production. The text for this choral play is on page 76.

▲ Make a Costume Hat

COSTUMES

Old Frost and Helpers: Have children dress all in white—white shirts, white or light pants, and white tights. Use oversized, unbelted, no-sew tunics made from white, gauze, chiffon, or silver fabric. You might want to glue cotton balls on some or all of the tunics. Consider also making simple hats from white fabric. Two right-angle triangles of fabric large enough to fit the child's head when glued together on the right-angle sides work well to make a simple elfin-type hat. Tape or staple white streamers (two to three feet long) onto pipe-cleaner necklaces and armbands, if desired.

Hanukkah Scene: Girls can wear any party dress. Boys should wear white or nice shirts and dark pants. Ties look good for boys.

German Christmas Scene: Children can wear nightgowns, pajamas, or robes over their regular clothes. They can carry storybooks or teddy bears, if desired. Sleep caps such as granny-type caps look nice.

English Christmas Scene: A formal look works well here. Boys wear white shirts and dark pants. Ties and suspenders are good additions, if available. Girls should be encouraged to wear their party best, with parent permission. The party clothes for this scene, however, should be of the traditional type with lace, satin, velvet, and floral being in order. No mod or pop colors should be worn. If girls want to wear long skirts with aprons or lace collars, this is fine, too.

American Christmas Scene: Children can wear regular clothes with scarves, hats, mufflers, and mittens. They should look as if they have been caroling on a cold December evening.

Mexican Christmas Scene: Again, have children wear white shirts and dark pants or skirts. If some girls have full bright-colored skirts or Spanish fiesta-style dresses, encourage them to wear these instead. Make tissue or crêpe-paper flowers in assorted bright colors for the girls' hair. Tie bright-colored sashes onto each child. Sashes should be 3 to 4 inches wide and 40 inches long for easy tying.

Chinese New Year Scene: If any children have Chinese pajamas, wraps, or kimonos, they should wear them. For those who don't, use bright red, yellow, or gold no-sew tunics belted at the waist with a black sash. White shirts and dark pants should be the costume base. If finances permit, you might want to decorate the edges of each tunic with metallic trim or fabric paint.

From *Practical Plays*, published by GoodYearBooks. Copyright ©1993 Pamela Marx.

SCENERY

Since the locale of the play changes with each scene, scenery is best if kept to the carry-on type. That is, often your props become the scenery. You might, however, have a small table available on the stage to accommodate a Christmas tree or money tree used in a particular scene.

Hanukkah: If you have access to a real dreidel and menorah, use these in the play. If you have no dreidel, let the children pantomime playing dreidel. If you have no menorah, make a menorah for a stage effect. The easiest way to do this is to cut one out of tagboard or posterboard. To ensure that it is sturdy enough for use as a prop, cut out two and glue them together. The classic menorah design is one of a horizontal bar sitting on a single base. The bar holds four candles to the right and four candles to the left of the center base, with one candle in the center sitting slightly higher than the rest. The menorah should be larger than life (about 12 by 18 inches) since it serves as both prop and scenery.

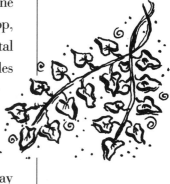

German Christmas: If a Christmas tree decorates your performance hall, you may be able to center this scene around your life-sized prop. If a tree is not available, a three-foot portable Christmas tree or a plywood Christmas tree can be carried onto the stage and placed on a small table. As an alternative, have a child wearing a long, green no-sew tunic act as your Christmas tree. Safety-pin a few decorations or bows on. A final alternative is to do without the tree and have the children pantomime the scene.

English Christmas: Children can carry on ivy and evergreen boughs, then pretend to hang and admire them. Actors playing children in this scene can hold and shake wrapped presents as though trying to guess what they contain. (Whenever possible, let children participate in the creation of these props.)

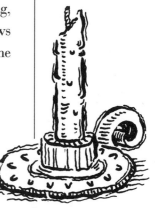

▲ Scenery

American Christmas: Scenery is not necessary for this scene. If you choose, carolers can carry music books from which they pretend to read and sing. Do this simply by folding black construction paper to look like a songbook.

Mexican Christmas: Children in this scene can carry a piñata or two, if available.

Chinese New Year: A life-sized dragon is called for in this scene. This is really both the scenery and the largest prop. Use a large piece of posterboard as the head of the dragon. Cut it in a shape appropriate to a dragon head so it is at least 24 to 30 inches in diameter. (The area around the dragon's eyes is often square in shape while the area around the mouth is more round.) Use two 2-1/2-inch-wide strips of tagboard taped onto the backside as handles. With markers, fabric, construction paper, and feathers, create a dragon face. Use red, gold, orange, and black accents to decorate the dragon's face.

For the body of the dragon, three or four children carry a length of fabric (over their heads) that is stapled to the dragon head. The fabric should be 24 to 30 inches wide and three to four yards long. As children "parade" the dragon, they should bend up and down at the knees so that the dragon undulates across the floor. Children should carry the fabric so that their heads and upper bodies are covered and only their legs show.

The dragon is followed by children shaking noisemakers, beating pots and pans, and perhaps carrying a dragon or two made like those on page 62.

Another piece of scenery for this scene is the money tree, which children can carry on stage. Fill an old coffee can with plaster, and insert an attractive branch. Wrap the coffee can in red tissue paper. Decorate the branches with crushed pieces of tissue (simulating flowers) and tiny red packages (simulating the wrapped money).

OLD FROST'S WINTER ADVENTURE STUDENT SCRIPT

PLAYERS

Old Frost
Winter Helpers (1 to 7)

HANUKKAH
Children (1 to 3)
Hora Dancers

GERMAN CHRISTMAS
Children (1 to 4)

ENGLISH CHRISTMAS
Mom/Dad (1 to 2)
Children (1 to 3)

AMERICAN CHRISTMAS
Carolers (1 to 4)

MEXICAN CHRISTMAS
Children (1 to 5)
La Raspa Dancers

CHINESE NEW YEAR
Children (1 to 5)
Dragon (needs at least 3 children)

PROPS

For ideas about props, refer to the suggestions under "Scenery" on page 65.

Curtain rises.

Enter Old Frost and Helpers with arms in the air, going in circles as though swept about by the wind. Old Frost can be either a boy or a girl.

Old Frost
Whoa! Cold winds are really blowing this winter. We've been swirling about so much, I've lost track of time and place.

Helper 1
I'll say, Old Frost. We've been blown right out of the Polar Ice Cap. Where are we now?

Old Frost
It's hard to say, but winter is a time of celebration the world over.

Helper 2
Maybe if we look in at that house, we'll know something about where we are or what time it is.

Hanukkah actors enter and freeze in place. Old Frost and Helpers "blow" themselves over to an imagined window. They brush snow away from the window, hold their hands up as though looking in, and watch.

Children in the Hanukkah scene begin to move. Several are playing dreidel on the floor. Several are gathered around the menorah and several are in either a line or circle (depending upon the number of children available) ready to dance the hora.

Hanukkah Child 1 (playing dreidel)
I'm so glad it's Hanukkah again.

Hanukkah Child 2
Yes, I love playing dreidel.

Hanukkah Child 1
You ought to. You always win.

Hanukkah Child 3 (around menorah)
When will it be time to light the menorah?

Child 3 motions to Child 1 and Child 2 to join him/her. They stand around the Child who holds the menorah.

Music begins and children sing "Hanukkah, O Hanukkah (Come light the menorah)" or another Hanukkah song with which you are familiar. (If you would rather not sing here, have children dance the hora *to recorded Israeli music. If the* hora *is too difficult, have children dance the simpler grapevine step.) While Children sing, the Dancers dance, either the* hora *or the grapevine step.*

When song ends, Hanukkah actors exit.

Old Frost
Boy, those children are sure enjoying their Hanukkah party.

Old Frost and Helpers begin to whirl about the stage again, with their arms in the air.

Helpers and Old Frost
Whoa! Whoa! Whoosh!

Helper 4

It's that North Wind again. Where is it taking us now?

Old Frost and Helpers whirl about the stage.

Helper 5 (pointing)

Look! What's going on down there?

Helper 6

It looks like we are in Germany. And it's Christmastime.

Helper 7 (a little smug or happy with self)

Did you know that Christmas trees originated in Germany?

Old Frost

How did you know that?

Helper 7

I read it in a book.

During this dialogue, the German Children enter the stage and freeze in their position around the tree.

Old Frost and Helpers wipe a viewing place in the window and look in. German Children begin to move as though they are decorating a Christmas tree.

German Child 1

I just love our tree this year.

German Child 2

Yes, it's beautiful.

German Child 3

I wonder who will be the first one to find the pickle on the tree and win the special surprise.

German Child 4

I found it! I found it!

Actors freeze. Chorus sings "Oh Christmas Tree." It's a nice touch if children can learn it in German.

German Children exit.

Old Frost and Helpers begin to whirl again.

Helper 1

Whoa! Here we go again.

Helper 2

What an icy wind! Where are we now?

Helper 3

I think we've blown over the English Channel to England.

Helper 4

Look! They are decking the halls inside.

During this dialogue, English actors enter and freeze in position. When Helper 4 cries "Look," English actors begin to pantomime. Parents hang boughs of greens. Children shake boxes and try to guess what's inside.

Old Frost and Helpers pantomime clearing the window pane and looking inside.

Mom/Dad 1

Oh, the holly and ivy look lovely this year.

Mom/Dad 2

Yes, let's put more holly on the mantle.

English Child 1

Can we have some mince pie?

Mom/Dad 1

Not now.

English Child 2

How about some plum pudding?

Mom/Dad 2

Not now.

English Child 3

How about just one little sugarplum?

From *Practical Plays*, published by GoodYearBooks. Copyright ©1993 Pamela Marx.

Mom/Dad 1 and 2 (jokingly, frustrated, facing audience with arms outstretched)

No. KIDS!

English actors freeze. Chorus sings "Deck the Halls."

English actors exit. Old Frost and Helpers begin to whirl. American carolers enter and freeze.

Helper 5

This wind is amazing. What is that down there?

Old Frost

Oh, that little puddle of water? That's the Atlantic Ocean.

Helper 6

No kidding. Where are we headed now?

Helper 7

I think we're on our way to the good old U.S.A.

Old Frost

Look now. It's Christmastime in America, too.

Carolers have entered and act as though they have just finished a song.

Caroler 1

That sounded great. What should we sing now?

Caroler 2

I know. Let's sing "Jingle Bells."

Caroler 3

Yes, let's. Everyone loves that one.

Caroler 4 (flapping arms around self)

Sing loud. It will help keep us warm.

Actors freeze. If one carries bells, the actor can ring them while the singers sing "Jingle Bells."

Carolers exit while Old Frost and Helpers begin to blow around again. Mexican actors enter and freeze.

Helper 5

Here we go again.

Helper 6

We've never been blown this far south before.

Helper 7

We're near the equator.

Helper 1

Look! That's Mexico down there and the people are celebrating *Las Posadas.*

Old Frost and Helpers freeze and look at the scene. Mexican actors act like they are gathered around the breaking of a pinata. One or two can carry a piñata on stage and set it down. One can carry maracas to use during the singing.

Mexican Child 1 (pointing in excitement)

Look! Juan just broke the piñata.

Mexican Child 2

Look at how much candy Maria got.

Mexican Child 3

Los Posadas parties are my favorite thing in the whole world.

Mexican Child 4 (hugging self in happiness)

I just love Christmas!

Optional: This dance segment is optional, but can be used if you choose to have another dance segment. Children can learn the Mexican folk dance La Raspa very easily. See page 55 for directions.

Mexican Child 5

They are starting to dance now. Let's watch.

Children designated as dancers begin to dance.

End of optional segment.

Mexican actors freeze. Chorus sings "Feliz Navidad" as popularized by Jose Feliciano, or "Duermete, Nino Lindo" from Children Sing Around the World *by Jerry Silverman, published by Mel Bay Publications, Inc., 1991. If maracas are appropriate to the song you choose, an actor now shakes the maracas during the song. (If children have performed* La Raspa, *you may choose to delete the singing in this scene.)*

Mexican actors exit and Old Frost and Helpers begin to whirl. Chinese New Year actors enter and freeze.

Helper 2

Oh, feel those warm winds.

Old Frost

Those winds are pushing us out fast. That's the Pacific Ocean we just passed over.

Helper 3

Look down there. It's another festival. Where are we now?

Helper 4

I think we are in China.

Helper 5

And it's the third day of the New Year celebration—the day for the dragon parade.

Some children are gathered around the money tree that one child is holding. Some are to the side of the stage as part of the dragon. They are surrounded by the Children with the noisemakers and pans.

Chinese Child 1 (holding money tree)

Did you see our money tree this year?

Chinese Child 2

It has so many gifts on it. That must be a good sign for the New Year.

Chinese Child 3

Listen. I think the dragon parade is coming. Open the door.

The dragon starts to undulate by. Children 1, 2, and 3 pantomime opening the door. They wave to the dragon. Children around the dragon speak before they beat pans and wave noisemakers.

Chinese Child 4

If we beat these pans loud enough, we will scare all the bad spirits away from the new year.

Chinese Child 5

That's just superstition.

Chinese Child 4

I know, but it's still fun.

The dragon crosses the stage and Children make noise. Scene freezes. Old Frost and Helpers begin to sway.

Old Frost

What a busy winter!

Helper 6

Yes, but I feel the warmer winds of spring blowing.

Helper 7

Yes, our winter work is done.

Old Frost

We've seen so many people from all over the world. Each shared the fun of celebration but each one celebrated in his or her own way.

Helper 1

The world's a beautiful sight when people are joyful and at peace.

All actors re-enter the stage. All sing "Let There Be Peace on Earth" or "I'd Like to Teach the World to Sing."

Curtain falls.

THE END

From *Practical Plays*, published by GoodYearBooks. Copyright ©1993 Pamela Marx.

The following is a shortened version of "Old Frost's Winter Adventures." It is suitable for use at holiday luncheons or other events at which a short (approximately 5-minute) show is appropriate.

Costumes, scenery, and props are about the same as for the longer play. Since this play is to be performed by a single class or a chorus, all holiday groups find their place in the staging area before the performance begins and Santa and the reindeer (or elves) move between them during the performance. The individual actor groups freeze when they are not speaking lines or singing.

Costume for Santa: Red no-sew tunic with a three-inch strip of fiberfill, quilting fill, or white fabric stapled onto the bottom of the tunic. Belt the tunic with a wide black sash. Wear a red triangle-type hat if no real Santa hat is available. Around the holidays, however, inexpensive Santa hats are usually available at drug stores or discount houses.

Costumes for Reindeer/Elves: Have these characters wear green no-sew tunics. Make antlers out of posterboard and affix them to a posterboard band around the children's foreheads, or make elf hats using the instructions for Old Frost's hat (page 64).

In this play, all actors are on stage in small groups between which Santa and his reindeer move during narration. Have the elves or reindeer lead Santa around the stage holding paper chains between them. You might want to reinforce the chain strips with masking tape.

SANTA'S BUSY NIGHT STUDENT SCRIPT

PLAYERS

Narrator
Santa
Reindeer or Elves

GERMAN CHRISTMAS
Children (1 to 4)

ENGLISH CHRISTMAS
Mom/Dad (1 to 2)
Children (1 to 3)

AMERICAN CHRISTMAS
Carolers (1 to 4)

MEXICAN CHRISTMAS
Children (1 to 3)

Narrator

On that first Christmas Eve so long ago, Santa loaded up his sleigh. Led by his trusty reindeer [or elves], Santa headed around the world to deliver his happy gifts. Everywhere he went, Christmas looked a little different.

Santa's first stop was in the British Isles. As he peered in window after window, Santa saw families with holly in hand decorating their homes. As they decorated their fireplaces and doorways and waited for Father Christmas to arrive, they sang.

Santa and reindeer make a trip around the groups of actors while the narration is read. When they stop at the English Christmas group, they pretend to brush away snow from the window to look inside. This should be done with a circular motion, and then they should hold their hands up to their eyes to pantomime looking through the window.

Mom/Dad 1
Oh, the holly and ivy look lovely this year.

Mom/Dad 2
Yes, let's put more holly on the mantle.

English Child 1

Can we have some mince pie?

Mom/Dad 1

Not now.

English Child 2

How about some plum pudding?

Mom/Dad 2

Not now.

English Child 3

How about just one little sugarplum?

Mom/Dad 1 and 2 (jokingly, frustrated, facing audience with arms outstretched)

No. KIDS!

All sing first two lines of "Deck the Halls." Santa moves around the stage during the narration and stops at the German group.

Narrator

Santa continued on his way and came to Germany. In each house he passed he saw a beautiful Christmas tree. Children were busy adorning tree branches with chains and stars and balls. As the children decorated, they sang.

German Child 1

I just love our tree this year.

German Child 2

Yes, it's beautiful.

German Child 3

I wonder who will be the first one to find the pickle on the tree and win the special surprise.

German Child 4

I found it! I found it!

All sing first two lines of "Oh Christmas Tree" in German, if possible. Santa moves around the stage to the American group.

Narrator

When Santa finished his work there, his reindeer led him over the Atlantic Ocean to the U.S.A. There the children gathered to carol in their neighborhoods and city streets. They sang a familiar song.

Caroler 1

We sounded pretty good on that one.

Caroler 2

Yes, "Silent Night" is a beautiful Christmas carol, but what should we sing now?

Caroler 3

I know! Let's sing "Jingle Bells." Everyone loves that one.

Caroler 4

Yes, let's. Sing loud.

All sing one verse of "Jingle Bells." Santa moves around the stage to the Mexican group.

Narrator

Once Santa had finished his busy work in the States, his sleigh carried him down to Mexico, where children gathered at *Las Posadas* parties to break piñatas, feast, and sing.

Mexican Child 1 (pointing)

Look! Juan just broke the piñata.

Mexican Child 2

Look at how much candy he got.

Mexican Child 3 (hugging self in happiness)

I just love Christmas and our *Las Posadas* parties!

All sing "Feliz Navidad" or other Mexican folk song of your choosing, such as "Duermete, Nino Lindo" from Children Sing Around the World *by Jerry Silverman, published by Mel Bay Publications, Inc., 1991. Santa moves around stage and to a general location you have chosen.*

From *Practical Plays*, published by GoodYearBooks. Copyright ©1993 Pamela Marx.

Narrator

Santa finished his sleigh ride around the world and headed back up to the North Pole. Santa had been busy but he felt good. He'd made many children all over the world happy that night. As Santa headed for the North Pole, he heard voices below and he, too, joined in.

Sing "We Wish You a Merry Christmas."

Narrator

Thank you for joining us on Santa's first ride, and happy holidays to all of you from all of us.

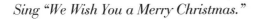

SUGGESTED READINGS

Babouschka and the Three Kings by Ruth Robbins. Parnassus Press, 1960.

The Best Christmas Pageant Ever by Barbara Robinson. Harper & Row, 1972.

The Channukah Tree by Eric Kimmel. Holiday House, 1987.

Gung Hay Fat Choy by June Behrens. Childrens Press, 1982.

Hershel and the Hanukkah Goblins by Eric Kimmel. Holiday House, 1989.

Lion Dancer by Kate Waters and Madeline Slovenz-Low. Scholastic, 1990.

Nine Days to Christmas by Marie Hall Ets. Viking Press, 1959.

The Polar Express by Chris Van Allsburg. Houghton Mifflin, 1985.

The Power of Light by Isaac Bashevis Singer. Avon Books, 1980.

HEARTS AND TARTS

Adventures in Mother Goose Land

A Valentine Play

This play, which centers around the stolen tarts of the Queen of Hearts, includes Mother Goose characters who participate in the search. In the course of the play, the Queen of Hearts and the children of Mother Goose Land ask passing characters from Mother Goose rhymes if they have seen the Knave. Finally, just as the King asks for his tarts, the repentant Knave enters.

WHY SHOULD CHILDREN PERFORM THIS PLAY?

This play can be performed straight or, with older children, "hammed up," resulting in a more campy performance. Younger children enjoy the rhymes, the images, and the sounds. Older children enjoy finding the humor in the rhymes.

This play can be performed as a Valentine play, but it also works just as well as part of an exploration of folk literature. Mother Goose rhymes are full of dramatic images of life and death, crime and punishment, good and evil. They are simple rhymes that are part of a great oral tradition, passed down from parent to child by the telling. To explore them tells us about ourselves and people everywhere—our fears, our joys, our sorrows, our angers.

Since a by-product of living in the telecommunications age is an unfortunate breakdown of the oral tradition, fewer and fewer children are familiar with many Mother Goose rhymes. This play and some of its activities open children up to a part of a long-standing oral culture they might otherwise miss.

HOW SHOULD I PREPARE CHILDREN FOR PERFORMING THIS PLAY?

There are many wonderfully illustrated Mother Goose rhyme books which you can make available to your children. Below are some classroom activity suggestions for exploring the rhymes.

PERFORMING ACTIVITIES

1. **Adopt-A-Rhyme.** Introduce this play as you would any play, but add one feature to your introduction. Some of the individual rhyme text in the play is abbreviated. As part of your introduction, read the entire text for each rhyme referred to in the play. To directly prepare children for the performance, ask

each child to "adopt" a rhyme. The child will be responsible for memorizing his or her adopted rhyme and presenting it orally to the class.

2. **Exploring History Through Rhymes.** Engage in a bit of historical meandering. Choose several rhymes that clearly evoke the time in which they originated. Many things in modern society are done differently than they were 100 to 200 years ago. We buy food in supermarkets. We wash and dry clothes in machines. We have complex delivery systems for water. Mother Goose rhymes can serve as a jumping-off point for discussions of the differences and similarities between life today and life in past centuries.

To discuss how life has changed, consider:

Bye, Baby Bunting	Ding Dong Bell
Jack Be Nimble	To Market, To Market
Jack and Jill	Polly, Put the Kettle On
Baa, Baa, Black Sheep	Little Polly Flinders

During your discussion invite children to envision daily life before there were cars, electric lights, running water and so many "modern conveniences" we take for granted today. Ask children to pantomime activities from "then" and "now." For example, children pantomime carrying water from the well (then) and turning on the faucet (now), or building a fire (then) and turning on the heater (now). These can be short all-class pantomime activities. Since the modern-day equivalent of historical practices often involves turning on a switch, children begin to see how much technology has freed us from many time-consuming tasks of yesteryear.

3. **Knavish Questions.** Due to the limitations of scripting text, while the Knave in the play has a change of heart and repents his evil ways in taking the tarts, there is no real discussion in the play of what led him to his change of heart. Have children discuss the character of the Knave.

▲ **Jack Be Nimble**

- Why might he have taken the tarts? Was it for a selfish reason or an unselfish reason? (Since he later repents, we can assume it was for a selfish reason.)
- Why might the Knave have had a change of heart? Did he see a crying child whose toy had been stolen? Did he remember lessons his parents had taught him about not stealing?
- Why is it bad to take other people's property without asking?
- How would you feel if someone took your backpack, toy, or book?

After class discussion, have children break into small groups, brainstorm a scene in which the knave changes his mind about his larcenous deed, and decides to return the tarts. To create these scenes, children will need to consider characters, script text, and staging.

WRITING ACTIVITIES

1. **Rhyme 'Round the World.** Explore folk literature from other cultures to help children see both the similarities and differences between the oral traditions in different countries. Try to find nursery rhymes from non-English speaking countries. One example contains Latin American rhymes: *Tortillitas Para Mama and Other Nursery Rhymes/Spanish and English* by Margot Griego, Betsy Bucks, Sharon Gilbert, and Laurel Kimball, illustrated by Barbara Cooney (Holt, Rinehart & Winston, 1981). Check with your local librarian or bookstore to see what is available in your area. After reading and talking about several nursery rhymes from another culture, ask children to write a paragraph or two telling the story of the rhyme in prose. This exercise allows them to think about what happens in the rhyme and retell it in their own words.

2. **Mother Goose Newspaper.** To get started on writing a class Mother Goose newspaper, ask each child to select a rhyme. Perhaps it will be their "adopted" rhyme. Then, to determine what types of articles should be in the newspaper, children can explore a real newspaper and its different sections: world news, local news, book and theater reviews, food, travel, sports, business, and weather. Children should think about their rhyme from the perspective of a story for one of these sections. (For younger children, you may need to specify the type of story they should try to write.)

Consider the following possibilities to get you started, but don't feel limited by these:

FOODS/RESTAURANTS

Pat-A-Cake	Sing a Song of Sixpence
Pease Pudding Hot	Little Jack Horner

SPORTS

Bye, Baby Bunting	Jack Be Nimble
This Is the Way the Ladies Ride	Here I Am, Little Jumping Joan
Here We Go 'Round the Mulberry Bush	

CRIME

Little Bo Peep

Three Blind Mice

Tom, Tom the Piper's Son

Who Killed Cock Robin?

Goosey, Goosey Gander

The Queen of Hearts

Taffy Was a Welshman

BUSINESS

See-saw, Marjery Daw

Hot Cross Buns

Peter Piper

To Market, To Market

Hickety-Pickety, My Black Hen

Baa, Baa, Black Sheep

TRAVEL

See-saw Sacradown, Which Is the Way to Londontown?

Doctor Foster Went to Glo'ster

When I Was a Bachelor, I Lived By Myself

Pussy Cat, Pussy Cat, Where Have You Been?

WORLD/LOCAL NEWS

Old Woman Who Lived in a Shoe

Old Mother Hubbard

Hush-a-Bye Baby on the Treetop

Three Little Kittens

Little Miss Muffet

Wee Willie Winkie

Little Polly Flinders

This Little Pig

Little Betty Blue

Jack and Jill

Little Bo Peep

The Grand Old Duke of York

▲ The Mother Goose News

SOCIETY

Rub-a-Dub-Dub

Georgie Porgie

Fiddle Dee Dee, Fiddle Dee Dee

Rock-a-Bye Baby, Thy Cradle is Green

Elsie Marley Has Grown So Fine

GARDEN

Mary, Mary, Quite Contrary

Ring a Ring of Posies

WEATHER

A Red Sky at Night

REAL ESTATE

The House That Jack Built

OBITUARIES

Solomon Grundy

Humpty Dumpty

MUSIC

Ride a Cockhorse

Cock a Doodle Doo

Little Boy Blue

Sing, Sing, What Shall I Sing?

Old King Cole

From *Practical Plays*, published by GoodYearBooks. Copyright ©1993 Pamela Marx.

S T A G E / T H E A T E R

Dance to Your Daddy	Dance, Thumbkin, Dance
Hey Diddle Diddle	Little Tommy Tucker

Some of the shorter rhymes (such as the one listed under "Weather") could be reprinted under the heading of the particular section with no further explanation. With the longer poems, though, try to have the children explore their rhymes by asking these questions:

- Who are the characters?
- Why do they do what they do?
- What will happen to them?
- What has caused them to be in the position in which they find themselves?

Part of the process of writing the article will be for children to "interview" the characters. They can do this by pairing up and role-playing. One child acts as interviewer; one acts as the character.

For example, consider this hypothetical interview:

Q. Polly Flinders, why did you sit by the fire?

A. *Because I was cold.*

Q. What happened when you sat there?

A. *I got my dress dirty.*

Q. Did you think about that before you sat by the fire?

A. *Yes, but I was cold.*

Q. After you warmed your feet, what happened?

A. *My mom came in and I got in terrible trouble.*

Q. Why?

A. *Because I got my dress all dirty in the cinders.*

Q. Will you do it again?

A. *No.*

Q. Well, how will you get warm the next time you are cold?

A. *I'll turn the heater on.*

Q. Do you have heaters?

A. *Oh, I guess not.*

(In this case, perhaps an interview can help children discover that there were no heaters as we know them when Polly sat by the fire.)

Answers can be sincere or silly. The article writer can sift out these things as he or she writes.

From *Practical Plays*, published by GoodYearBooks. Copyright ©1993 Pamela Marx.

CROSS-CURRICULAR ACTIVITIES

1. **Classroom Cookery.** Here are some recipes to start you off as you explore rhymes:

C H E R R Y   T A R T S (such as the ones the Knave stole)

1-1/4 cup granulated sugar   4 eggs, slightly beaten
3 8-ounce packages cream cheese, softened
1 box vanilla or chocolate wafer cookies
2 cans cherry pie filling

• Preheat oven to 350°.
• Mix together cream cheese and sugar. When soft and well mixed, add eggs slowly, stirring with a large fork. (When children make this recipe, you sometimes end up with a very lumpy cream mixture. Don't worry, because it still bakes up surprisingly well.)
• Using aluminum cupcake liners (or paper ones in muffin tins), place a single wafer cookie at the bottom of each liner. Cover with a tablespoonful of cream mixture.
• Bake for 25 to 30 minutes. Remove tarts and cool.
• Drop a teaspoonful of pie filling on top of each tart and top with a whipped topping of your choosing, if desired.

An easier version of this tart is to fill each one with instant vanilla pudding before topping with cherries.

P U D D I N G (as in "Pease Pudding Hot")

Pudding can be made the easy way or the easiest way.

Easy Way
Make cooked pudding from a mix using a hotplate. This is fairly easy and children can see that the pudding thickens as it cooks and then cools, going from "pease pudding hot" to "pease pudding cold."

Easiest Way
Make instant pudding by the shaking method, which is fun to do. Place all ingredients into a plastic container with an airtight lid, and allow children to take turns shaking the pudding. Once everyone has been given a turn, let the pudding rest for ten minutes and serve.

▲ **For Plum Cake**

PLUM CAKE (as in "To Market, to Market")

Here are two plum cake recipes. One is really a biscuit; the other is a cupcake.

Plum Surprise Cakes

4 cups self-rising flour   2/3 cup real mayonnaise

2 cups milk   3 tablespoons sugar

Plum jam

- Mix all ingredients except jam.
- Spoon a layer of batter into greased muffin tins (about 1/3 full).
- Spoon in a teaspoon of plum jam or a thin slice of peeled plum.
- Spoon in more batter so tin is 1/2 to 2/3 full.
- Bake at 400° in a preheated oven for 15 to 20 minutes or until golden in color.

Makes 24 muffins. Before you add jam or plum, make sure you have stretched your batter as necessary to make the needed number of cakes.

Plum Pot Cakes

2 slightly beaten eggs   1-1/4 cup strawberry yogurt

1 package yellow cake mix   Plum jam

- Mix all ingredients except jam and spoon into paper-cup-lined muffin tins until 1/2 to 2/3 full.
- Place 1 teaspoon of plum jam in the center of each and bake in a 350° oven for 25 to 30 minutes or until a toothpick comes out clean. Makes 24 to 28 muffins.

2. **Castle Creations.** Using a cereal box and two paper towel tubes, children can make the castle of the King and Queen of Hearts for classroom or bulletin board display.

- Wrap the boxes and tubes in butcher paper or gray construction paper. Tape or glue one paper towel roll to each side of the cereal box.
- Cut circles of black or red construction paper, and slit the circles to the middle to make turret roofs for each paper towel tube.
- Glue small construction-paper flags to toothpicks and insert them into the roofs and/or along the top of the cereal box.
- Mark the paper with crayon or markers so it looks as if the castle is made from stones or bricks. Draw a drawbridge or great door in the center of the cereal box.
- Decorate with hearts for the King and Queen of Hearts.

▲ **Create a Castle**

3. Rhyme Guessing Game. If you can locate a coloring book or other simple pictures of Mother Goose rhymes, place them on a board without their respective poems. Have children play a guessing game. Which rhyme does each picture illustrate? Can the children tell? How can they tell? They need to look for key ideas or clues in the pictures.

Another way to play this game is to have children draw pictures of the rhymes they "adopt" (as suggested in the Performing Activities in this chapter). Remind children to draw key objects from their rhymes. For example, any picture of "Hickory Dickory Dock" would have a mouse and a clock in it. If the picture is not self-explanatory, help children see the key elements of the picture so that they can guess the rhyme to which it relates. This game is best played after children are familiar with each other's rhymes. This activity helps children identify props and/or pantomime ideas that are essential to acting the part of a rhyme character in the play.

How should I stage this play?

This play can be produced with a large number of children or with a handful. If you plan to produce it with a few, merely delete Mother Goose characters from the passing parade, and have children double up on the repetitive lines of the Mother Goose Land Children. If you have many children, you might want to add characters from other rhymes or use rhymes that can accommodate many actors, such as "The Old Woman Who Lived in the Shoe." Remember how many children she had? Also, there is nothing magical about the rhymes chosen for this play. If you believe other Mother Goose poems would be of more interest to your children, or if you prefer to have children pick their own, feel free to substitute your choices.

An additional production suggestion concerns the character of the Knave. As the play is now written, the Knave does not appear until the end. You might consider whether you want the knave to "steal" on- and off-stage on tiptoe at odd moments, always carrying his tray of tarts. This could add a humorous element to the play. For example, while the Queen is wringing her hands, the Knave could be tiptoeing this way or that. Make sure everyone on stage is looking away from the direction of the Knave as he tiptoes by.

▲ **Guess Who I Am!**

COSTUMES

Children of Mother Goose Land: These characters can dress in nightgowns or bathrobes carrying assorted stuffed animals.

Rhyme Characters: For boys, use white, long-sleeved shirts and black pants as the costume base. Add plain-colored no-sew tunics with belts to give the look of nursery-rhyme illustrations. They can also wear hats that they may have at home. Avoid baseball or other modern hats. Girls should try to wear long skirts, aprons, bonnets (or straw or sunhats) and ruffled shirts. No-sew tunics can be cut ankle length for girls who need or want to wear long skirts but have none.

The King, Queen, and Knave: These characters should wear no-sew tunics and should have some red in their attire. You can give them the heart effect by pinning red or white hearts on their tunics or other costume clothing. The Queen should have a long skirt. Both the King and Queen should wear paper crowns. The Knave can wear the triangle hat described on page 64.

SCENERY

If you choose to use scenery, consider a castle scene. One method would be to paint a simple masonry wall scene on a large banner and hang it at the back of the stage. To further this effect or to create a castle effect, have children make a "castle" framework at each side of the stage using two sets of boxes—three boxes for each side. Pile the three boxes on top of each other, largest to smallest.

Paint the boxes gray or cover them with newsprint. Paint black mortar lines so the boxes look like mortared stones. Glue a large heart to each box structure to signify the King and Queen of Hearts.

HEARTS AND TARTS STUDENT SCRIPT

PLAYERS

Queen of Hearts
Little Miss Muffet
Polly Flinders
Mother Hubbard
Knave of Hearts
Other Children of Mother Goose Land

Jack Horner
Dr. Foster
Jack Be Quick
King of Hearts
Children (1 to 14)

PROPS

Let the rhyme itself guide you about props. For example, Jack Be Quick can carry a candlestick, Mother Hubbard can carry her dog (or the leash that is tugged from off-stage), and Jack Horner can carry his pie. The Knave, of course, can carry a cookie tray of tarts. Props are not necessary, but you and the actors may find ways to use them to humorous advantage.

Curtain rises.

The Children of Mother Goose Land enter, giggling and whispering, and settle themselves to one side of the stage. Queen of Hearts enters shaking her head and wringing her hands. She stops in a designated stage position (probably to the side of center) and begins to speak.

Queen of Hearts

I'm the Queen of Hearts
I made some tarts
All on a summer's day.

But the Knave of Hearts
He stole those tarts
And took them clean away.

Oh, children, children, I must know.
Where is that knave? Where did he go?

Children

Dear Queen, we've looked this way and that.

As Children say "this way and that," they look in unison and dramatically to the right and then to the left with their hands up to their foreheads, as though searching the horizon.

Children

We do not know where the knave is at.

Child 1 (rising and pointing, if desired)

Here comes Jack Horner.
Maybe he knows.

Enter Jack Horner.

Child 2

Little Jack Horner, do you know?
Where is the knave? Where did he go?

Jack Horner

I'm little Jack Horner,
I sat in a corner
Eating a holiday pie.
I put in my thumb
And pulled out a plum,
And said, "What a good boy am I!"

Queen of Hearts

But, Jack Horner, from your corner,
Did the knave you spy?

Jack Horner

Oh no, not I. Tah, tah. Goodbye.

Exit Jack Horner.

Queen of Hearts (with disappointment)

Oh my.

Child 3

Do not be sad, my Queen, today.
Here comes Miss Muffet.
What does she say?

Enter Little Miss Muffet.

From *Practical Plays*, published by GoodYearBooks. Copyright ©1993 Pamela Marx.

Child 4

Little Miss Muffet, do you know?
Where is the knave? Where did he go?

Little Miss Muffet

I'm little Miss Muffet,
I sat on a tuffet
Eating my curds and whey.
Along came a spider
And sat down beside me,
And scared me clean away.

Child 5

But, little Miss Muffet, from your tuffet,
Did the knave you spy?

Little Miss Muffet

Oh no, not I. Tah, tah. Goodbye.

Exit Little Miss Muffet.

Queen of Hearts (wearying)

Oh my.

Child 6

Don't be sad, my Queen, today.
Here comes Dr. Foster.
What does he say?

Enter Dr. Foster.

Child 7

Dr. Foster, do you know?
Where is the knave? Where did he go?

Dr. Foster

I'm Doctor Foster.
I went to Glos'ter
In a shower of rain.

I stepped in a puddle
Up to my middle.
I'll never go there again.

Child 8

But, Dr. Foster, when in Glos'ter,
Did the knave you spy?

Dr. Foster

Oh no, not I. Tah, tah. Goodbye.

Exit Dr. Foster.

Queen of Hearts (wringing her hands)

Oh my.

Child 9

Don't be sad, my Queen, today.
Here comes Polly Flinders.
What does she say?

Enter Polly Flinders.

Polly Flinders

I'm little Polly Flinders.
I sat by the cinders
Warming my pretty toes.

(If desired, Polly can raise a long skirt to expose not "pretty toes," but monster feet.)

Child 10

But, Polly Flinders, by those cinders,
Did the knave you spy?

Polly Flinders

Oh, no, not I. Tah, tah. Goodbye.

Exit Polly Flinders.

Queen of Hearts (holding her head in her hands)

Oh my.

Child 11

Don't be sad, my Queen, today.
Here comes Jack Be Quick.
What does he say?

Enter Jack Be Quick carrying a candlestick.

Jack Be Quick

I'm Jack be nimble
Jack be quick
Jack jump over the candlestick.

For a humorous interlude, have Jack put the candlestick down and attempt to jump over it, falling down, then sitting up and scratching his head. He could then say, "I never can seem to get that right."

From *Practical Plays*, published by GoodYearBooks. Copyright ©1993 Pamela Marx.

Child 12

But, Jack Be Quick, by the candlestick,
Did the knave you spy?

Jack Be Quick

Oh no, not I. Tah, tah. Goodbye.

> Exit Jack Be Quick.

Queen of Hearts

Oh my.

Child 13

Don't be sad, my Queen, today.
Here comes Mother Hubbard.
What does she say?

> Enter Mother Hubbard.

> *Mother Hubbard is holding a rope that is attached to something unseen off-stage. There can be a little "tug of war" with the leash for humorous effect, if desired.*

Mother Hubbard

I'm old Mother Hubbard.
I went to the cupboard
to get my poor dog a bone.

But when I got there,
The cupboard was bare,
And so the poor dog had none.

Child 14

But, Mother Hubbard, in that cupboard,
Did the knave you spy?

Mother Hubbard

Oh no, not I. Tah, tah. Goodbye.

> Exit Mother Hubbard.

Queen of Hearts (rubbing her eyes dramatically with her fists)

Boo hoo, boo hoo.
What will I do?
The king is calling now.

> King of Hearts enters, patting
> his stomach in a grandiose way.

King of Hearts

My queen, my queen, oh I am near.
Where are those tarts you made, my dear?

Queen of Hearts (drying eyes)

I'm the Queen of Hearts,
I made some tarts
All on a summer's day.

The Knave of Hearts
He stole those tarts,
And took them clean away.

King of Hearts (stomping about)

I'm the King of Hearts
Where are those tarts?
I'll beat that knave full sore.

Queen of Hearts (looking off-stage, surprised and happy)

Oh no, my king,
Please don't be mean.
Here comes the knave—
He's on the scene.

*Queen points off-stage as Knave enters carrying the
tray of tarts. Knave has his head cast down.
He knows he did wrong.*

King of Hearts

See here, you knave,
Stand up, look brave,
And tell us the truth, not lore.

Knave of Hearts

I'm the Knave of Hearts.
I stole the tarts
And took them clean away.

But I was wrong, I know that now.
I seek my pardon. Tell me how.

King of Hearts (taps his chin thoughtfully and paces; then he points his finger in the air as a thought comes to him)

Knave of Hearts, for your part,
Learn this lesson well.

Both day and night, do only right.
Keep others straight as well.

All actors on stage freeze. Only the Children of Mother Goose Land speak. These lines can be divided up or spoken in unison.

Children of Mother Goose Land (in unison)

From that day on,
Knave did no wrong.
He learned his lesson well.

"Do what is right
With all your might"
To others he did tell.

Curtain falls.

THE END

SUGGESTED READINGS

Chinese Mother Goose Rhymes by Robert Wyndham. World Publishing Company, 1968.

Granfa' Grig Had a Pig and Other Rhymes without Reason from Mother Goose by Mother Goose. Little, Brown, 1976.

Marguerite de Angeli's Book of Nursery and Mother Goose Rhymes by Marguerite de Angeli. Doubleday, 1954.

Old Mother Hubbard and Her Dog by Sarah Catherine Martin, illustrated by Paul Galdone. McGraw-Hill, 1960.

Tortillitas Para Mama and Other Nursery Rhymes by Margot Griego, Betsy Bucks, Sharon Gilbert, and Laurel Kimball. Holt, Rinehart & Winston, 1981.

The Rainbow People
A Community Play

This play illustrates the common bonds between all people regardless of their differences. People have basic needs for food, water, and shelter. Important also is the human need to find acceptance and friendship.

In the play, Red, Blue, and Orange People pass by the house of the Purple People, seeking shelter. The Purple People dismiss these passersby simply because they look different. A great storm breaks and destroys the house of the Purple People. They run for cover to the house of the Green People, who have already given shelter to the others who came their way. Even though the house is full, the Green People open their door a bit wider and welcome the Purple People.

WHY SHOULD CHILDREN PERFORM THIS PLAY?

"Rainbow People" is a play about the needs that are common to all people. It is also a play about the error of judging people on their appearance, specifically on whether they seem to be the same or different from ourselves. These issues are important ones to be explored at all grade levels and in all communities.

In urban areas, the United States is fast becoming a plural society. Immigrants from many parts of the world live together. Sometimes the cultural differences between people lead to misunderstandings, dislikes, and tensions. Teaching children the importance of sharing and enjoying our differences as well as our similarities is valuable at an early age to help foster intercultural trust and understanding.

The play can also be used as a jumping-off point for discussion of other differences between people. People look different from one another: they have different hair, eyes, heights, and skin. But people also have different skills and abilities. Some people have physical disabilities, such as sight or hearing loss. The challenges of life with limited sight or hearing or other physical limitations can be addressed.

This play provides an opportunity to explore the themes of community and the wrongfulness of prejudice, whether based on skin color, religious beliefs, or physical disability. The play and the other activities in this chapter illustrate these lessons for children.

HOW SHOULD I PREPARE CHILDREN FOR PERFORMING THIS PLAY?

Many of the activities in this chapter, which explores the themes of community and cooperation, can and should be done in pairs or groups. The focus of the play and many of the suggested activities is the similarity between all people regardless of gender, race, religion, or ability.

PERFORMING ACTIVITIES

▲ **A Pantomime Play**

1. **Pantomime Play.** Have children team up to pantomime actions or activities that can help bring about peace. As a class, brainstorm some action verbs about peace—that is, actions that will make the world a more peaceful place. Some of these might be: share, help, give, and work. Perhaps you will want to be more specific, using words such as "grow food," "help an older person," "comfort someone who is sad," or "speak out for peace."

   Divide the class into two teams. Assign each team (or have them pick from a hat) one or more of these words or phrases. One team acts out the word or phrase (without using words, as in charades). The other team must guess the phrase. This exercise helps prepare children for the pantomime requirements of the play.

2. **Get Inside the Heads of the Purple People.** As part of play preparation, have children investigate the behavior of the Purple People as characters. In the script, their unwillingness to open their door to those who knock is only briefly explained. One reason they give is that they do not know the passing people. Another reason they give is that the passing people are different from themselves. Ask the children to explore why the Purple People might respond this way. Here are some discussion questions for starters:

   - Are the Purple People afraid of the others? If so, why?
   - Is it because the passersby are different from the Purple People?
   - Do the Purple People think the others are better or smarter than themselves?
   - Do the Purple People think they are better than the passersby? If so, why? If not, why not?
   - Have you ever felt uncomfortable around someone different from yourself? Someone older, perhaps? Why?
   - In what ways are people different?
   - How are people alike?

Ask children to break into small groups to organize, script, and perform short scenes in which the Purple People discuss whether or not to let the passersby in.

3. **Character Pantomimes.** Have children pantomime the actions of the play's characters. The different color groups in the play carry different props. One group carries bundles of sticks. Others carry jugs of water or baskets of food. As an occasional brief exercise during classroom hours, have the children stand in their places and pantomime carrying sticks on their shoulders or heavy jugs of water. When the travelling groups arrive at the Purple People's house and ask for shelter, they are tired, cold, and hungry. How can the children show these feelings in the way they carry their props? Have children pantomime walking in the cold or walking into a strong wind. Have them pantomime the house crashing down on them, as happens to the Purple People in the play. Ask those children who do a good job of pantomiming to show the rest of the class how they act out these feelings and actions.

As a further exploration of the characters in the play, have children work in groups to create short pantomime skits about one of these groups. For example, the Orange People carry sticks. Children could pantomime scenes in which the Orange People carry the sticks, lay them down, build a fire, and feel the fire's warmth. The Blue People carry jugs of water. Children could pantomime a group activity involving carrying water, resting, pouring, and drinking water. These group pantomime activities can be done by any group of students, not just those who perform particular parts in the play.

WRITING ACTIVITIES

1. **Peace Acrostic.** Brainstorm with children a very short thought about peace. It can be very simple such as "Peace Now" or "One People," or you can simply use the word "Community," "Peace," or "Rainbow." Then, letter by letter, have the children think of words that explain peace and put them in a sentence next to the appropriate letter.

Examples:

P is for patience in working with others.
E is for everyone getting along together.
A is for always trying to work out our differences.
C is for caring for others.
E is for each of us being part of the world family.

P Put our arguments behind us.

E Everyone must try to get along.

A Answers to peace come when we try to find them.

C Caring for each other is a peaceful thing to do.

E Everyone needs love.

After you have created a class acrostic, ask children to create their own to different words or phrases.

2. **Friendly Cinquains.** Give each child the name of another child in the class. Each child will write a positive poem about the child whose name he or she received. Perhaps children will want to explore the cinquain poem structure with this exercise.

Cinquain construction is like this:

Line 1: Two syllables (Use the persons' name or, if it is a one-syllable name, write "Our Jim," or a noun describing the person.)

Line 2: Four syllables (These could be adjectives describing the person, or a four-syllable phrase.)

Line 3: Six syllables (Use adjectives or verbs that describe the person.)

Line 4: Eight syllables (Use a phrase that describes some idea or feeling about the person.)

Line 5: Two syllables (Use a noun about the person if you used his or her name in Line 1. If you did not, use his or her name here.)

Examples:

Good Friend

Loving, Caring

Very kind and thoughtful

She sent me cards when I got sick

Nikki

Matthew

Happy, Friendly

Caring, Helping, Growing

He gets along well with others

A Friend

▲ **Hands Art**

Younger children might prefer writing a rhyming couplet about friendship. Have them write a two-line poem. Children can decide whether each line should have three, four, or five syllables. Before the children begin, give them some help by listing or brainstorming with them some words with the theme of getting along with one another. Sample words are: share, care, give, peace, love, kind, joy, happy, hands, heart.

Examples:

Love means share.
Share means care.

Let's hold hands
Through all lands

When arguments cease
Then we will have peace.

CROSS-CURRICULAR ACTIVITIES

1. **Hands Art.** Use black sheets of construction paper (11" x 18") as the background for this project. Have children trace their hands on different-colored papers and cut out the outlines. Children should cut out four pairs of hands. Each pair can be a different color. Glue the hands onto the black paper to make a design of the students' choice. This project can be done in groups using larger sheets of black paper. (If this project is done in groups, ask each child in a group to cut two pairs of hand shapes out of one color only. Each child will then work with the other children to create the final design.)

2. **Alike and Different.** A couple of simple classroom activities can be useful in highlighting both the ways in which people are alike and the ways in which people are different from one another.

For younger children: Get three eggs in different-colored shells and/or different sizes. White, brown, and speckled chicken eggs should be readily available. Ask the children to look at them. They each look a little different in color, in shape, in smoothness. But when the eggs are broken, each is the same on the inside. This

▲ **Alike, yet Different**

is like people. We all look a little different, but inside we are the same. We have blood and teeth and bones. We have things that make us happy and things that make us sad. We are more alike than different. Apples (green, red, and yellow) can be used for this exercise instead of eggs. If you use these food examples, follow it up with another cooperative activity such as cooking (scramble eggs or cook applesauce).

For older children: We often hear of people referred to by words like black, white, or brown. What does this mean? These words can be confusing. When children roll up their sleeves and compare their hands and arms, they see that no two people have exactly the same color skin. No two shades are alike. This exercise can help foster an appreciation of the uniqueness of each person. When this is followed with a discussion of how we are alike, children can gain a new sense of understanding.

3. **Explore Other Languages.** Teach children words, phrases, or songs in another language. As children struggle to learn words or songs in another language and make sense of them, they begin to understand the struggle of an immigrant in a new country. Not only are places, foods, and customs new, a whole new language must often be learned. For songs from other countries, see *Children Sing Around the World* by Jerry Silverman published by Mel Bay Publications, Inc., 1991; *Folksongs from the Far East* by Peter Gritton, published by Faber Music, 1991; and *Folksongs from Africa* by Malcolm Floyd, published by Faber Music, 1991.

You might also try to teach children some words, phrases, or songs in sign language. Perhaps an expert in sign language could visit your class to demonstrate how to say words and phrases.

▲ **Sign Language**

How should i stage this play?

Staging and costuming on this play are very straightforward. Three character groups and four groups of "weather" actors enter and exit. The remaining two character groups remain largely stationary. This play works very well if performed by two classes, one older and one younger. The younger group can perform the "weather" parts. Or the "weather" actor parts can be deleted and the changes in weather handled solely by the other actors' lines and pantomime.

▲ **Make a Hat!**

COSTUMES

Color Group Characters: Use no-sew tunics in the color of the character. Using white shirts and dark pants as the costume base, have each costume group wear appropriately colored no-sew tunics—such as Purple People wearing purple no-sew tunics.

If you have extra fabric, make hats with glue and two fabric triangles. Use two right-angle triangles of fabric for each hat. The triangles should be large enough so that, when the two sides that make up the right angle are glued together, the "hat" that is formed fits comfortably on the child's head.

Other costumes can be made as follows:

White Clouds: Use white no-sew tunics for the clouds. Cut the tunics larger than usual so that when the actor spreads his or her arms out from the shoulder, the tunic nearly reaches his or her wrist. Then use marker to create a fluffy cloud effect.

Chill Winds: Use gray, regular-sized no-sew tunics, or have children wear white. Then staple gray crêpe-paper streamer strips to pipe-cleaner necklaces that they can slip over their heads. Pipe-cleaner armbands with streamers attached can also be used. Keep arm streamers to no more than two feet in length.

Black Clouds: These costumes can be made the same way as those for the White Clouds, except that you will use black cloth and add the cloud designs with white chalk. You might want to tape or glue foil lightning bolts to the tunics.

Rain: Use gray or blue no-sew tunics with blue and gray crêpe-paper streamer strips attached at the shoulders or to pipe-cleaner necklaces.

Rainbow: The rainbow can be a child wearing a multicolored no-sew tunic, or it can be a child holding a large posterboard rainbow.

SCENERY

For sets or scenery, the main elements are the two house structures. One will be purple, and one will be green. While the opening and closing of doors can be pantomimed, it is useful to have some symbolism of the houses on stage. Cutting a window frame shape out of a large piece of posterboard and affixing it to a curtain or wall will give this sense.

A storm occurs toward the end of the play. This should be dramatized in some way to show the destruction of the purple house. Have someone shake the window frame if it is attached to a moveable article like a curtain. If this cannot be done, make sure the Purple People dramatize the collapse of their home by covering their heads, waving their arms, and pushing against the imaginary walls.

This play uses a lot of pantomime, which can be a great deal of fun for children. The more they use their bodies in the pantomime and practice the effects called for by the play (as described on page 98), the more effective they will be during the play's performance.

THE RAINBOW PEOPLE STUDENT SCRIPT

PLAYERS

Narrator
Red People (1 to 7)
Blue People (1 to 7)
Orange People (1 to 7)
Purple People (1 to 7)
Green People (1 to 5)

White Clouds (optional)
Chill Winds (optional)
Rain (optional)
Black Clouds (optional)
Rainbow

PROPS

Red People: They carry heavy baskets of food. Place a few carrots or squash in the baskets. If baskets are not available, fold lengths of burlap and tie them with string to create bags, or fill brown paper bags with crumpled newspaper and tie them shut. When children carry the bags, they pantomime that they are heavy.

Blue People: They carry jugs of water. Have children bring plastic milk or water jugs and containers, canteens, or any other type of container that would give the effect of carrying water.

Orange People: They carry bags or bundles of sticks. Several of the Orange People can carry the burlap bags described above for the Red People. Several should carry small bundles of tied sticks.

Curtain rises.

The Purple People are at place on stage.

Narrator

On a day when the breeze blew softly and the clouds drifted slowly, the Red People wandered down the road carrying heavy baskets of food.

The Red People enter.

Red 1

Ah, it's a lovely day.

From *Practical Plays*, published by GoodYearBooks. Copyright ©1993 Pamela Marx.

Red 2

Look at the beautiful clouds.

If there are actors to portray Clouds, they enter and sway from side to side as they move gracefully toward the exit point of the stage.

Red 3

Yes, the clouds are beautiful, but these baskets of food are getting heavy.

Red 4

And I'm tired and thirsty.

Red 5

Look, there's a purple house up ahead. Maybe we can rest there.

The Red People walk toward the purple house and knock on the door. The door opens.

Red 6

Hello. Can we come in and rest?

Red 7

We are tired and thirsty.

Narrator

The Purple People looked at the Red People. Then the Purple People looked at each other.

Purple 1

No, you cannot come in.

Purple 2

We do not know you.

Purple 3

You look different to us.

Purple 4

Be on your way.

The Red People shrug their shoulders, look sad, and exit.

Narrator

And so the Red People went sadly on their way. But soon the Blue People wandered down the road carrying jugs of water.

The Blue People enter carrying jugs of water.

Blue 1

What a nice day!

Blue 2

Yes, but a chilly wind is beginning to blow.

If there are actors to portray the Chill Winds, they enter. Waving arms in unison, they make whooshing sounds until they exit the stage area. Blue People shiver and cry "Brrrr."

Blue 3

These jugs of water are getting heavy.

Blue 4

We are all tired and hungry.

Blue 5

Look, there's a purple house up ahead. Maybe we can rest there.

The Blue People knock at the door. The door opens.

Blue 6

Hello. Can we come in and rest?

Blue 7

We are tired and hungry.

Narrator

The Purple People looked at the Blue People. Then the Purple People looked at each other.

Purple 1

No, you cannot come in.

Purple 2

We do not know you.

Purple 3

You look different to us.

Purple 4

Be on your way.

From *Practical Plays*, published by GoodYearBooks. Copyright ©1993 Pamela Marx.

The Blue People shrug their shoulders, look sad, and exit.

Narrator

And so the Blue People went sadly on their way. But soon the Orange People wandered down the road carrying bundles and bags of sticks.

Enter Orange People carrying their bags and bundles.

Orange 1

Oh, the winds are blowing hard now.

Orange 2

The winds are so cold, they bite my skin.

Chill Winds enter again.

They wave arms in unison and "whoosh" louder than at their last entrance. They move toward the exit while the Orange People pantomime their fight against the wind. The Orange People put arms to their heads and slant their bodies forward as they walk.

Orange 3

These sticks are getting heavy.

Orange 4

And we are all tired and cold.

Orange 5

Look, there's a purple house up ahead. Maybe we can rest there.

All Orange People

Oh, I hope so. I hope so.

The Orange People knock on the door. The door opens.

Orange 6

Hello. Can we come in?

Orange 7

We are cold and hungry.

Orange 1

And a terrible storm is coming.

Narrator

The Purple People looked at the Orange People. Then the Purple People looked at each other.

Purple 1

No, you cannot come in.

Purple 2

We do not know you.

Purple 3

You look different to us.

Purple 4

Be on your way.

The Orange People shrug their shoulders, shiver, and exit sadly, but quickly, in the cold wind.

Narrator

And so the Orange People went sadly on their way. And just as they left, the chill winds turned icy. The drifting clouds turned black. Thunder clapped and rain pounded the earth.

If there are actors portraying the storm, Black Clouds and Rain enter, waving their arms wildly. Off-stage, pot lids, cymbals, and drums beat out the sound of a wild storm. Black Clouds and Rain surround the purple house. The window shakes and the Purple People look frightened. If you do not use actors to portray the storm, pot lids and cymbals can still crash off-stage while the Purple People pantomime the storm and the house coming down on them.

Purple 5

Oh, no. The storm is tearing our house apart.

All Purple People

Run! Run for cover!

During this time, Black Clouds and Rain find stage positions throughout the stage area, remain in position, and wave their arms to simulate a storm. The Purple People exit hurriedly through Black Clouds and Rain and head toward the Green House. Black Clouds and Rain exit elsewhere simultaneously, or if no exit is available, they sit.

Narrator

And so the Purple People ran down the road looking for shelter and help. Soon they saw a green house.

The Purple People can move back and forth across the stage while the Green People enter and set their stage position.

Purple 2

Look, there is a green house up ahead.

Purple 3

Maybe the people there will help us.

The Purple People knock at the door and it opens.

Purple 6

Hello. Can we come in?

Purple 7

We are cold and wet and tired.

Narrator

The Green People looked at the Purple People. Then the Green People looked at each other.

The Purple People shiver and look worried.

Green 1

Well, we shared our home with the Red People, and they shared their food with us.

Green 2

Yes, and we shared our home with the Blue People, and they shared their water with us.

Green 3

And we shared our home with the Orange People, and they shared the warmth of a fire with us.

Green 4

Our home is very full.

Green 4 pauses, and the Purple People look worried.

Green 4

Still, our door can always open a bit wider.

Green 5

Come in. Share our food and warm yourselves by our fire.

Purple People

Oh, thank you. You are so kind.

Green 1 (pointing)

Look! The storm is clearing!

> Enter Rainbow at side of stage.

Green 2

And you can see the rainbow.

All actors look toward the Rainbow.

Purple 1

It's as though all the colors in the world joined hands to stand up there side by side.

Green 3

Yes. How beautiful a rainbow is with every color, side by side, bending over the earth in peace.

Narrator

And that day the Purple People learned a very big lesson about living. Never again did they close their door against another, whether red, blue, green, or orange. They had learned about the beauty of the rainbow.

Curtain falls.

T H E   E N D

SUGGESTED READINGS

The Big Book for Peace edited by Ann Durell and Marilyn Sachs. Dutton Children's Books, 1990.

The Gold Cadillac by Mildred Taylor. Dial Books, 1987.

The Handmade Alphabet by Laura Rankin. Dial Books, 1991 (sign language alphabet).

Knots on a Counting Rope by Bill Martin, Jr., and John Archambault. Henry Holt and Company, 1987.

Let the Celebrations BEGIN! by Margaret Wild and Julie Vivas. Orchard Books, 1991 (concentration camp survival).

Matthew and Tilly by Rebecca Jones. Dutton Children's Books, 1991.

Molly's Pilgrim by Barbara Cohen. Lothrop, Lee & Shepard, 1983.

A Picture Book of Martin Luther King, Jr. by David Adler. Scholastic, 1989.

THE PICNIC

The Picnic
An Environmental Play

This play has an environmental theme. It can be performed in conjunction with Earth Day festivities or as a twist on the "green" theme for St. Patrick's Day. In the play, a group of children who are on a picnic hike around a park to discover dirty lakes, pollution-covered flowers, and frightened animals. The children resolve to take immediate steps to remedy the environmental mess they find.

WHY SHOULD CHILDREN PERFORM THIS PLAY?

The challenges of our environmental problems are apparent to anyone who picks up a newspaper or listens to a newscast. This play touches on four areas of environmental concern—air, land, water, and animal life—and challenges children to make a difference.

Education about environmentally sound habits needs to start with children. We teach them to be caretakers of our Earth by helping them view their daily activities from an Earth-safe perspective. Can this container be recycled? Why are there so many layers of packaging on that product? Do we need to use chemical pesticides?

This play, especially when presented and prepared using the suggestions in this chapter, meshes well with a science-based environmental unit, and it can help bring environmental awareness to the forefront of a child's mind. It will also act as a catalyst for analytical thinking about practices at home.

HOW SHOULD I PREPARE CHILDREN FOR PERFORMING THIS PLAY?

This section provides many different ideas for educating children in the area of environmental awareness and for preparing them to present a play on our world's environmental woes. With the information they gain, they will become effective spokespeople for our Earth.

PERFORMING ACTIVITIES

1. **Healthy Planet Pantomimes.** Place the children in small groups, and ask them to think about environmental problems they have seen or experienced. After discussing these problems within the groups, each group decides on one environmental problem to portray in a scene to the class. For example, children can role-play their reactions to:

    -   a littered park, in the center of which they find an empty trash can
    -   an adult pouring paint or dirty motor oil into the gutter
    -   a fellow student tossing recyclable paper into the trashcan

    Remind children that to do the role-play successfully, they will have to decide what happens in their scene, who the characters are, what props they will need to use, and appropriate staging.

2. **Earth Speak.** If you have children create environmental alphabets or Earth haiku as suggested in the Writing Activities (page 114), ask them to present their alphabet letters or poems to the class. Use this exercise to have children practice speaking slowly, clearly, and loudly.

3. **Words for Our Earth.** Have children research environmental terms that may be new to some or all of them. This research can be as simple as using a dictionary. Ask children to present to the class their findings and answer any questions that the definition or research raises. Five or six children can make their presentations each day for a week until all the children have had an opportunity. Remind children to make eye contact with the audience and to speak slowly and loudly. Ask each child in the class to maintain a notebook of these "Earth Words." With each presentation, a new group of words and information about them is added to the notebook. In this way, environmental topics are reinforced.

▲ **Earth Speak**

Some possible research words and phrases are:

Environment	Pollution
Toxicity	Ecology
Energy	Resources
Conservation	Landfill
Recycle	Solid Waste
Biodegradable	Compost
Litter	Emissions
Smog	Ozone
Manufacturer	Acid Rain
Atmosphere	Phosphates
Groundwater	Sewage
Leachate	Aqueducts
Pesticides	Oil Spills
Endangered	Extinct
Habitat	Species
Environmental Protection Agency	

WRITING ACTIVITIES

1. **Environmental Alphabets.** After the children have become familiar with the general issues of environmental concern, they may be ready to create an environmental alphabet. To create an environmental alphabet, students think of an environmental word or concept for each letter of the alphabet.

Depending on the abilities of your students and the available time, you can have each child create a complete environmental alphabet or you can divide up the letters between the children. The alphabet example on page 115 centers on one theme. This is not necessary, however. Each letter can be devoted to any environmental subject if that is easier for children (and it usually is).

The children can make posters of their alphabet concepts and present them in conjunction with the play performance. Making the alphabet poster allows a child to think about an environmental concept and to reflect that thought in the poster.

RECYCLING ABCs

A All

All of us can help recycle. You can help, too.

B Bottles

Bags

Recycling means bottles and bags,

C Cans

Cartons

cans, and cartons are used again.

D Dumps

We need to recycle because our garbage dumps are getting full.
Recycling saves room.

▲   **Environmental
Posters**

E Energy

Environment

Earth

Recycling also saves energy. All these things are good for the environment.

F Foam

Many things can be recycled. Foam can be recycled.

G Glass

Glass can be recycled, too.

H Habit

Recycling is a good habit.

I Involve

Involve your family in recycling.

J Jars

Can your family recycle something by using it again in your home? Ask
Mom and Dad if they can reuse old jars by storing things in them. They
will appreciate your help.

▲ Make Your Own Environmental Posters ▼

K Kindness

Recycling is an act of kindness to our Earth.

L Landfill

There are lots and lots of other things you can recycle. Remember, recycled things don't go to a landfill.

M Metal

How many more things can you think of to recycle? What about metal cans? Can metal be recycled?

N Newspapers

What about newspapers? Can newspapers by recycled?

O Often

Recycle these things often. Better yet, recycle them all the time.

P Plastic

Plastic bottles and bags can also be recycled.

Q Questions

Ask questions about recycling. Does your city have a recycling program? Does your school?

R Recycling

Responsibility
Resources
Recycling is everyone's responsibility. It saves natural resources.

S Save

When we save resources, we save growing things and flowing things and things that are inside the Earth.

T Tree

A tree is a natural resource. It is a growing thing. Trees are cut down to make paper.

U Useful

We should try to save trees because they are useful to both people and animals.

V Variety

For one thing, a great variety of birds and animals make homes in trees or find food from them. We also need trees to help make the air good for us to breathe.

W Water

Water is a natural resource. It is a flowing thing. Using old things over again helps save water and energy.

X X-Ray

What can you find to recycle? Put on your extra-special x-ray recycling eyes and look around.

Y You

If you do, you will become an important helper to our Earth.

Z Zip

When you find those recyclables, gather them up. Ask Mom and Dad to zip over to the recycling center to turn them in. Try to recycle everything from A to Z.

▲ **Environmental Posters**

2. **Environmental Newsletter.** The environmental alphabet could also be a starting point for publishing an environmental newsletter. Such a newsletter can include student interviews with principals or local officials on school or city environmental programs, poems, essays on recycling and Earth Day, as well as interesting facts relating to the environment which the children can collect from a variety of sources—library books, school books, newspapers, magazines, and local museums.

3. **Earth Haikus.** Have children make up haiku poetry in celebration of the Earth and its needs. A haiku has three lines. The first line has five syllables, the second line has seven syllables, and the third line has five syllables. The lines do not rhyme. They can each be separate sentences, or the entire poem can express one thought.

Examples:

Clouds are very gray
Skies are the color of smoke
Because we pollute.

Earth trembles and sighs
As land, air, and water die
Drowning heaven's cries.

Today is a day
For thinking about the Earth
And what I can do.

CROSS-CURRICULAR ACTIVITIES

In addition to routine preparation for play performance, you can undertake some special activities that will serve to enhance a child's understanding of the issue raised by the play. Three "field studies" are described below. The first one focuses on air quality. The second focuses on litter and water pollution. The third one focuses on biodegradability, the burgeoning landfill problem, and the need to recycle.

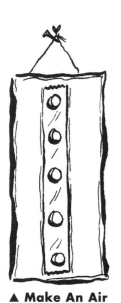

▲ Make An Air
Quality Analyzer

1. **Air Quality Activities.** An air quality survey for your community is an easy, but enlightening, proposition for children. Collect empty plastic margarine or frozen whipped topping containers. The containers should be white or clear. Smear the inside of each container with petroleum jelly. Mark the outside with the address of the child who will take home the container. Have the children take the containers home or distribute them to friends and local businesses. They should be hung in a tree or under an eave for two weeks to one month. When they are returned, analyze how dirty the petroleum jelly is. What made it dirty? Are some samples dirtier than others? Why is this? Is there a freeway or factory nearby?

   Another version of this activity is to punch four sets of holes in 5-x-2-inch strips of posterboard. Have children run clear tape down one side of each strip to cover the holes. Ask children to hang the strips in their homes and yards for two to four weeks. The exposed tape should collect the various types of dust and dirt in the air in their homes and yards.

2. **Water Quality Activities.** Another good survey is a litter survey. This survey can demonstrate how much simple litter can collect on just one short segment

of a street or other designated area. If we consider that litter of this type is picked up by water run-off and carried to bodies of water far away from the place the litter is dropped, we begin to see how much damage our collective litter can do.

For this survey, choose a fifty-foot stretch of gutter or a discreet park, playground, or other open area. Collect the litter in and near the designated area each day for one week. What kinds of things do you collect? Can these hurt local animals, both those passing by the area and those in any waters to which the litter is carried? How can papers, plastics (six-pack tops), balloons, and metal be harmful to animals?

Any discussion of water pollution should include a discussion of pesticide use and how run-off and underground seepage can contaminate both above-ground and underground water. Ask children to think about other things that can adversely affect bodies of water. For example, what is bad about detergents that contain phosphates? What is bad about oil spills? How can these hurt the Earth's water?

In this vein, another good activity is to have children research the laundry detergents and whiteners they use at home. Make a classroom chart. How many of the detergents and whiteners used contain phosphates? Talk about phosphates and the problems they pose for naturally occurring waters.

3. **Waste and Landfill Activities.** A biodegradability study can be very illuminating. Have the children choose twenty or thirty items such as paper clips, pencils, paper, plastics, whole apples, apple cores, pennies, aluminum cans, and cloth. Package some of the paper in sealed plastic bags. Make sure you include samples of whole fruit and damaged or sliced fruit. Bury the samples for one month in an area that gets some water, either by rain or sprinkler. When you unearth your treasure trove, consider which things show signs of decomposition. Are there differences in the amount of decomposition you see, depending upon how items were buried?

▲ **What Is Biodegradable?**

This biodegradability study helps demonstrate the difficulty of our waste and landfill problem and reinforces the importance of recycling and changing our buying habits.

4. **Environmental Exhibit.** Create an exhibit to share with the school, local library, or a community center. Any or all of the three surveys described above can provide an informative exhibit for students or members of the community during Earth Day-type celebrations.

▲
Create Environmental Exhibits
▼

Another activity that also yields samples for an exhibit table is a comparative shopping expedition. Ask students to look for products such as rice, pastas, chili, hot cereals, applesauce, and fruit cocktail. They should try to find these products packaged in their simplest form and in their most layered form (as they usually are for microwave cooking or school lunches). Encourage children to question why we purchase one over the other. Does it really take that much longer to heat something up on the stove versus in the microwave? Do we need to carry applesauce to school in a disposable plastic cup, or can we use a reusable container instead? Are changes in the more wasteful practices worth it if they help save landfill space and resources?

HOW SHOULD I STAGE THIS PLAY?

This play is relatively short and is best staged for assembly or public performance purposes if coupled with some introduction of the environmental subject matter. One presentation format for the play is:

- Opening remarks: Welcome and brief statement of environmental concern. A child could write this statement. He or she might explain why the performance is being held and why he or she thinks it is important.
- Presentation of environmental alphabet: Each child enters holding and showing his or her poster and restating its text into a microphone. Once the alphabet posters have all been presented, the children pass them to the end of each student row to be collected.
- Song or statements of several interesting environmental facts collected by the children.
- Performance of the play
- Song

Obviously, you can delete any of these elements to fit your preparation or performance time needs.

The play itself can be staged in one of two ways. If you have a large number of children to accommodate, plan to have eight to fifteen picnickers. The picnickers will leave the central picnic area in small groups, each group heading to a different environmental zone. If you have a small group, two or three children can be the picnickers and they can move from zone to zone. The actors in each zone can double up on parts, and/or you can delete any extraneous parts.

COSTUMES

For younger children: Consider simple posterboard "costumes" that are held up to the face. For example, large water-drop shapes with face cut-outs can serve as costumes for the "water" actors. Or you can use fish shapes with face cut-outs. Christmas or evergreen trees with face cut-outs can serve as the costumes for the "plant" actors, and flower shapes for the "flower" actors. Make one side of each flower gray or brown. When the flower actor is dusted off (as described in the play), he or she can flip the costume to a bright-colored underside. The animals can have large animal-shaped heads such as bears and rabbits.

For older children: Use more intricate paper-cut-type masks as the costumes for the "animal" and "water" or fish actors. No-sew tunics in the appropriate body color can also be worn. For example, the no-sew tunic for the lake actors would be blue. The plant zone actors can wear green no-sew tunics with paper cups, fast food containers, and paper trash pinned to them. The flower actors can simply wear brightly colored or floral no-sew tunics with pipe-cleaner necklaces of black crêpe-paper streamers. These streamers are dusted off (or taken off and placed on the floor) at the proper moment during the play. Children who play the picnickers can simply wear some exaggerated sport or casual clothing. Hats are a great idea. Headgear can include baseball caps, visors, sunhats, and scarves.

SCENERY

If you have tree scenery such as tagboard trees attached to chairs, the actors can sit and stand in and around the trees. You can also use a painted mural of a nature or park scene as background scenery. The mural can be hung at the back of the stage.

THE PICNIC STUDENT SCRIPT

PLAYERS

Children (1 to 15)

Flowers (1 to 5) (also referred to as "Flower Zone")

Fish or Waterdrops (1 to 6) (referred to as "Water Zone")

Trees (1 to 4) (referred to as "Plant Zone")

Animals (1 to 6) (referred to as "Animal Zone")

PROPS

Blanket

Basket

Paper plates

Curtain rises.

Children 1 to 15 are center stage, around the picnic blanket. They sit or stand on and around the blanket with a basket and plates as though eating. The other four actor zones are scattered as space permits around the stage. When curtains open, the actors are all in place.

Note: For a less static opening, have the environmental zones in place with the picnicking children entering to set up their picnic before the script action begins. This can be done without dialogue (as a pantomime), or encourage children to come up with their own opening lines which would lead into the lines below.

Child 1

Oh, I love going on a picnic.

Child 2

Yes, this was a great idea. I like being outside with the trees and animals.

Child 3

This is a beautiful place. Look at the trails around us.

Child 1

Let's go explore.

All Children

Great idea! Let's go!

If you have ten to fifteen picnickers ("large group" direction), they should break off in groups to the flower, plant, animal, and water zones. If you have only two or three picnickers ("small group" direction), these children should walk to the flower zone to begin their nature exploration.

Child 4 (arriving at the flowers first)

Look over here. Look at these flowers.

Child 5

Hey, you flowers are all dusty and brown. How did this happen to you?

Flower 1

The air in this city is very dirty.

Flower 2

There are too many cars, and people drive everywhere. They never think to walk.

Flower 3

And many factories spew great clouds of smoke into the air. It falls on our petals and leaves.

Flower 4

Even people in their homes hurt the air around us. They use sprays and pesticides and chemicals that get into the air and land on us.

Flower 5

But what are we to do? We are just simple flowers.

Child 6

This is terrible. See here, when you dust off your petals, you are beautiful underneath.

Children 1 to 6 "dust" off flowers while flower actors either take off their streamer necklaces or flip their tagboard costumes over, as appropriate.

For a small group, one picnicker runs to the water zone; other picnickers follow after he or she calls out. For a large group, picnickers already at the water zone signal to others and call out. Picnickers at the other zones turn, look, and listen.

Child 7

Look, look over here at the lake.
The water is all stagnant and mossy.

Child 8

And, look, there's litter floating under the surface. How did this happen?

Fish or Waterdrop 1

People take the waters on this Earth for granted.

Fish or Waterdrop 2

They use detergents with phosphates. When these phosphates get into our water, they make too much algae grow.

Fish or Waterdrop 3

And this makes lakes unhealthy. When lakes get unhealthy, many fish die.

Fish or Waterdrop 4

Sometimes people change their car oil and dump it where they shouldn't. Then it gets into the water and hurts fish.

Fish or Waterdrop 5

And many people use pesticides and other poisons to kill weeds and bugs. Rainwater and run-off carry these poisons from the land to lakes and seas.

Fish or Waterdrop 6

But what are we to do? We are just simple fish (or waterdrops).

Child 8

This is terrible.

Picnickers talk among themselves, looking concerned.

For a small group, one picnicker runs to the plant zone. Other children follow after first child calls out. For a large group, a child at plant zone calls out to all others who turn, look, and listen.

Child 9

Look, look over here at this grassy meadow and the trees. It is dirty and full of trash.

Child 10

How did this happen?

Tree 1

People. It's always people. They are not careful.

Tree 2

They have a picnic and they leave papers and cups on the ground.

Tree 3

Or they take a walk into this meadow drinking a soda and toss the can on the path.

Tree 4

But what are we to do? We are just simple trees.

Child 10

This is terrible!

Picnickers again talk among themselves, looking worried.

For a small group, one child moves to the animal zone and calls out. Others follow after the call. For a large group, one child at the animal zone calls out to others. Picnickers at other zones turn, look, and listen.

Child 11

Look over here. These animals are trembling in fright.

Child 12

What's happened to you?

Animal 1 (trembling)

Oh, life in the wild is getting harder and harder.

Animal 2

People destroy our homes when they build new buildings and roads.

Animal 3

They leave litter around that cuts and hurts us.

Animal 4

Sometimes we even mistake litter for food. When we try to eat it, we get sick or worse.

Animal 5

Some people chase us to try to make pets out of us, but when they put us in cages, we get sick and die.

Animal 6

But what are we to do about it? We are just simple animals.

Child 12

This is terrible.

All picnickers return to the central picnic area. They are pondering what they have seen and heard, talking to each other, shaking their heads, and looking very concerned.

Child 13

Yes, it's all terrible. But what can we do about it? We are just children.

Child 14

These are big, big problems, but many big problems are made by lots of little mistakes.

Child 15

Yes, like litter. If everyone just cleaned up his or her own trash, we could solve the litter problems.

Child 13

Let's make a start today.

All Children (except one)

Yes, let's! No more litter!

One child remains unconvinced. He comes to center stage shaking his head.

Child 1

But that's not going to help much. Our Earth has too many problems for us to make a difference.

Child 2

Well, it's a beginning, and we can do much more. We can be careful about the products we buy.

Child 3

Yes, we can buy more natural products and avoid ones with chemicals.

Child 4

And we can recycle glass and metal and plastic so we save natural resources.

Child 5

All these little things can add up to a big difference.

Child 6

If we don't try to change now, the world won't be a very nice place to live in when we grow up.

Child 1

Yes, you're right. Let's start now. At least we can try to make a difference.

All Children

Yes, let's do it now. Let's help save our Earth!

All Flower, Water, Plant, and Animal Actors (cheering)

Yeah! All right!

Close with song. Any song with an environmental theme can be used here. The Beach Boys' "Don't Go Near the Water" is one such choice. The following can also be sung (to the tune of "Jim Along Josie"):

The Earth is ours. We must protect it.
Do your part. Let's start today.

Name the problem. Find an answer.
Step by step, let's start today.

Let's clean up, now. Don't be careless.
No more litter. Change today.

Let's recycle. We can do it.
Glass and paper. Change today.

Change your habits for our Earth, now.
Do your part and start today.

The following is sung to the tune of "Yankee Doodle Dandy":

Mother Earth has lots of problems
You and I helped cause them.
So it's time for us to act
Let's make a helping hand pact.

Help the Earth
Do what you can.
Make recycling your plan.
Help the Earth
Look here and there
And show how much you care.

Children can also make up their own lyrics to a standard melody.

Song ends and actors call out:

One Actor

We will do our part.

All Actors (pointing at audience)

Will you?

Curtain falls.

THE END

SUGGESTED READINGS

Brother Eagle, Sister Sky by Chief Seattle. Dial Books, 1991.

The Great Kapok Tree by Lynne Cherry, Harcourt Brace Jovanovich, 1990.

Keepers of the Earth by Michael Caduto and Joseph Bruchac. Fulcrum Publishing, 1988.

The Lorax by Dr. Seuss. Random House, 1971.

Mighty Tree by Dick Gackenbach. Harcourt Brace Jovanovich, 1992.

A River Ran Wild by Lynne Cherry. Harcourt Brace Jovanovich, 1992.

Who Really Killed Cock Robin? by Jean C. George. Penguin Books, 1984.

The Wump World by Bill Peet. Houghton Mifflin, 1970.